WITNESSES OF THE LIGHT

DANTE

WITNESSES OF
THE LIGHT

BEING THE

𝔚illiam 𝔅elden 𝔑oble 𝔏ectures

FOR 1903

BY

WASHINGTON GLADDEN

WITH PORTRAITS

Essay Index Reprint Series

 BOOKS FOR LIBRARIES PRESS
FREEPORT, NEW YORK

First Published 1903
Reprinted 1969

CT
105
E5
1969

STANDARD BOOK NUMBER:
8369-1081-8

LIBRARY OF CONGRESS CATALOG CARD NUMBER:
77-84307

PRINTED IN THE UNITED STATES OF AMERICA

CONTENTS

THE WILLIAM BELDEN NOBLE LECTURES

THIS Lectureship was constituted a perpetual foundation in Harvard University in 1898, as a memorial to the late WILLIAM BELDEN NOBLE of Washington, D. C. (Harvard, 1885). The deed of gift provides that the lectures shall be not less than six in number, that they shall be delivered annually, and, if convenient, in the Phillips Brooks House, during the season of Advent. Each lecturer shall have ample notice of his appointment, and the publication of each course of lectures is required. The purpose of the Lectureship will be further seen in the following citation from the deed of gift by which it was established : —

"The object of the founder of the Lectures is to continue the mission of William Belden Noble, whose supreme desire it was to extend the influence of Jesus as the way, the truth, and the life ; to make known the meaning of the words of Jesus, 'I am come that they might have life, and that they might have it more abundantly.' In accordance with the large interpretation of the Influence of Jesus by the late Phillips Brooks, with whose religious teaching he in whose memory the Lectures are established and also the founder of the Lectures were in deep sympathy, it is intended that the scope of the Lectures shall be as wide as the highest interests of humanity. With this end in view, — the perfection of the spiritual man and the consecration by the spirit of Jesus of every department of human character, thought, and activity, — the Lectures may include philosophy, literature, art, poetry, the natural sciences, political economy, sociology, ethics, history both civil and ecclesiastical, as well as theology and the more direct interests of the religious life. Beyond a sympathy with the purpose of the Lectures, as thus defined, no restriction is placed upon the lecturer."

I

DANTE, THE POET

The " Divina Commedia " is of Dante's writing, yet in truth it belongs to the Christian centuries; only the finishing of it is Dante's. So always. The craftsman there, the smith with that metal of his, with his tools, with these cunning methods — how little of all he does is properly *his* work! All past inventive men work there with him ; — as, indeed, with all of us, in all things. Dante is the spokesman of the Middle Ages ; the Thought they lived by stands here in everlasting music. — *Carlyle.*

Dante is the greatest prophet of the Christian centuries, because he has given utterance to the largest aggregation of truth, in terms of universal experience, and in a form permanent through its exceeding beauty. — *Charles Allen Dinsmore.*

> Ah, from what agonies of heart and brain,
>   What exultations trampling on despair,
>   What tenderness, what tears, what hate of wrong,
> What passionate outcry of a soul in pain,
>   Uprose this poem of the earth and air,
>   This mediæval miracle of song!
>
> *Longfellow.*

WITNESSES OF THE LIGHT

I

DANTE, THE POET

" It is intended," says the Founder of this
Lectureship in her deed of gift, " that the
scope of the Lectures shall be as wide as the
highest interests of humanity. With this end
in view — the perfection of the spiritual man
and the consecration by the spirit of Jesus
of every department of human character,
thought, and activity — the Lectures may
include philosophy, literature, arts, poetry,
the natural sciences, political economy, sociology, ethics, history, both civil and ecclesiastical, as well as theology and the more direct
interests of the religious life." Under such
a charter one's liberties are large, and I shall
be quite within the precept if I devote the
hours which we shall spend together to the
study of the lives of a few men who have

stood forth, in generations widely separated, as representatives of the truth that was in Jesus, as witnesses of the light that lighteth every man coming into the world. Not one of these men was professionally or distinctively a religious teacher; some of them would have found it difficult to pronounce any of the formularies by which the various ecclesiasticisms test their adherents; but not one of them could have been the man we have known or could have uttered the message that was given to him but for the presence in his life of that Spirit whose incarnation Jesus was. It is because the work of these men was done quite outside the realm of organized Christianity that I have selected them; their lives illustrate the truth that the kingdom of heaven is larger than the visible church.

I have called them witnesses of the light. This may seem a superfluous function; is not the light its own best witness? It would be, doubtless, if there were not so many caverns and cellars in which men can hide themselves from it; if there were not so many who walk abroad wrapped in the darkness of tradition or superstition or fear. So it happens that it is a great part of the business of God's

messengers in this world to point to the light.
Of the Forerunner it was said, " The same
came for witness, that he might bear witness
of the light, that all might believe through
him.   He was not the light, but came that he
might bear witness of the light."   And Jesus
said of himself, in the one testimony which
most clearly defines his mission : " For this
cause was I born, and for this came I into the
world, that I should bear witness to the truth."
No new truth needs to be created or invented;
there is enough and to spare, and that which
it is most needful for us to know lies upon
the threshold of our lives ; we do not have to
climb to heaven after it or to descend into the
depths to unearth it ; it is near us, — so near,
oftentimes, that we do not see it ; and the
mission of prophet and seer and teacher is to
bring home to us realities of the homeliest
sort, whose meaning we too often miss ; to
open our eyes to the environing beauty which
appeals to us in vain, and to speak the word
which shall arouse in us the slumbering sense
of things unseen and eternal.

The witnesses whom we are about to call
in these studies uttered their testimony in
four different languages, and brought to the

world messages greatly varying in form; but
we shall find the unity of the spirit under-
lying all this variety of expression, and shall
have reason, I trust, to rejoice in the light
into which they have guided our feet.

Let me say, also, that these lectures are
not for scholars. I am not an expert in literary criticism; I can offer no help to the
well-instructed student of any of the litera-
tures into which we shall look; all that I
hope to do is to gather up and set in order
some of the more obvious facts respecting the
life and work of these great men, that un-
learned people, like myself, may get a little
better idea of the place they filled and the
work they did.

Of Dante the poet we are now to speak.
It would be difficult for the best instructed
teacher to present, within the limits of one
short discourse, any adequate account of this
man or of his works. The books which have
been written about Dante now run up into
the thousands; three large octavo volumes
are filled with titles and descriptions of the
Dantesque literature. You could not read, in
two or three lifetimes, all that has been writ-

ten to illustrate the character and expound
the teaching of this one man.

It is a little curious to note the rise and
fall of the current of popular interest in
Dante. After his death a chair was founded
in his native city for the exposition of his
great poem in the Duomo; and on the walls
of that sanctuary his picture was painted by
Michelmo; they still show it to you near the
great portal, though age has blurred its out-
lines and faded its colors. Boccaccio, who
was eight years old when Dante died, was
the first occupant of that chair, and his lectures were given fifty-two years after Dante's
death. Other Italian cities followed the example of Florence; at Bologna, Pisa, Pia-
cenza, and Venice popular instruction was
given respecting his great epic; and at Milan
an institution was founded by Archbishop
Visconte, to expound its mysteries. Not only
in Italy was Dante renowned. English bish-
ops wished to read the Comedy, and, moved
by their request, an Italian bishop rendered
it into Latin. The sixteenth century saw
twenty-one editions of this poem; the seventeenth forty-two; the eighteenth four; of the
nineteenth I have not the full tale. A his-

torian who counted the translations in 1843
reported nineteen Latin, twenty-four French,
twenty English, twenty German, two Spanish.
Since then the list of English translations has
been considerably extended. Three of the
best of these have been made in America,
that of Thomas W. Parsons, that of Longfellow, and the exquisite prose version of Professor Charles Eliot Norton.

The fact that the eighteenth century produced only four versions of the great poem
against forty-two in the seventeenth and a
greater number in the nineteenth illustrates
the intellectual activity of the eighteenth century. It was a mocking age, whose prophet
was Voltaire, and this is Voltaire's flippant
judgment: "The Italians call him divine,
but it is a hidden divinity; few people understand his oracles. He has commentators,
which, perhaps, is another reason for his not
being understood. His reputation will go on
increasing because scarce anybody reads him."
This does not throw much light on Dante, but
it helps us to estimate Voltaire.

It is evident, then, that we have before us
to-night one of the great characters of Christian history; one whose genius has exacted

from the thinkers and the readers of six centuries a larger tribute of attention than has been given perhaps to any other poet who has lived within that period. No one who cares to know what influences have shaped modern thought can afford to be wholly ignorant of Dante.

His life began in Florence, in the month of May, in the year 1265. The beautiful Tuscan capital on the banks of the Arno was then a mediæval town much smaller than to-day, and with few of the treasures of art which it now possesses. The commercial spirit was well developed, and the long and bitter strife between the feudal and the commercial classes was already raging.

These Italian communes or republics of the Middle Ages present a most interesting study. The industrial and trading classes had gathered in the cities and had developed a rude sort of democracy, — not a radical sort of democracy, to be sure, — much the same sort that our New England fathers set up when they graded the seats in their meeting-houses according to " rank, state, and dignity," assigning the best pews in the synagogue to those of most social distinction, and putting their plebeians in the back seats. Thus these Italian communes usually had a consulate of their most distinguished men, who administered municipal affairs, supported by a grand council of one hundred or so of their illustrious citizens. Below these was a parlemento, or town-meeting, to which all adult citizens belonged. But the business was done mainly by the consuls and the grand council; the popular assembly did not exercise much power.

In castles, round about these cities, had dwelt the nobles, holding their lands for the most part as fiefs under the Holy Roman Emperor, who was always a German. Their presence was to these sturdy burghers an obstruction and a menace. The land which they occupied was needed for the sustenance of those who dwelt within the walls, and the nobles nearest the cities were gradually forced by the townsmen to abandon portions of their estates, and to dwell for at least a part of the year within the walls. Here they became a disturbing element; industry of all sorts was beneath them, and Satan found plenty of mischief for their idle hands; feuds were fierce and perennial.

The internal condition of these Italian cit-

ies was most lamentable.   Security there was
none for life or property.   The commune had
failed ; democracy was unequal to the task of
preserving order — in communities ignorant
and brutal as these it always is ; the dictator
must be called in.   Some noble, generally from
another city, was chosen chief justiciary, and
these despots, who confirmed their power by
courting the populace, were often bloodthirsty
tyrants.   In Mr. Symonds's words, " They
had all the selfishness of an aristocracy, none
of its nobleness.   They combined the suspi-
cious, intriguing spirit of party leaders with
the ferocity of brigands and the inhumanity
of autocrats.   Each despot was jealous of his
neighbor, cruel to his kin.   Domestic tragedies, poisonings, imprisonments, treacheries,
frauds of guardians, oppressions of the weaker
by the stronger member of a ruling house,
were encouraged by the facility of revolution
which the peculiar constitution of semi-repub-
lican, semi-despotic governments afforded, in
the midst of hungry competitions and rival
states." [1]

Not only did the cities thus organize for
themselves a lively Pandemonium within their

----

[1] *An Introduction to the Study of Dante*, p. 29.

own walls, but their relation to one another
heightened this disorder. There was no union
among them; no recognized bond of a common nationality; the hand of every city was
against every other. Wars were incessant.
For territory, for commercial primacy and
privilege, for all the prizes of independent
statehood they were always fighting.

Through the tumult of these streets and
the strife of jealous municipalities another
distracting note is constantly sounding — the
battle-cry of the Empire against the Papacy.
Each asserted a supremacy which the other
denied, and the struggle between them is the
tragedy of the Middle Ages. Into this conflict the Italian cities — with quarrels enough
of their own, one would think — were constantly drawn. The nobles, as feudatories
of the Emperor, were generally his partisans;
the free cities, for the most part, were the al-
lies of the Pope. The Papacy, in those early
days, appeared to be the champion of democracy; and those who sought to reform the
abuses of the church were disposed to take
the side of the Emperor, so that it might be
stated as a general rule that religious liberals
were good imperialists and political liberals

were good papists. There was a tendency, however, for every community to divide on this question of Pope and Emperor; and by this strife cities were torn asunder — each party on coming to power was likely to banish the chiefs of the opposite party, to tear down their palaces and confiscate their estates.

Such was the state of sunny Italy when Dante Alighieri was born. His family was one of aristocratic lineage; there may have been a Teutonic strain in the blood; castles were theirs without the walls, and towered houses within. " On Arno's beauteous river, in the great city, I was born and grew," is the poet's own report. When he was nine or ten years old his father died; his education went on under the tutorship of Brunello Latini, a great scholar of that day, with whom he studied rhetoric, poetry, and mathematics, — gaining also a good knowledge of several of the Latin classics, Vergil, Lucan, Ovid, and Statius. Music and painting were also among his accomplishments. Without doubt he was a studious and serious lad, beyond his years in many ways, capable of great experiences; for it was before his father's death, when he was

only nine years old, that something happened
to this boy that the world has remembered for
six centuries and will never forget. His father took him to a May party at the house of
one of his rich neighbors, Folco Portinari,
and there for the first time he saw Beatrice
Portinari, the daughter of the house, a little
girl of eight. See how vivid is his memory
of that meeting as he recalls it many years
after : —

" Her dress on that day was of a most noble color, a subdued and goodly crimson, gir-
dled and adorned in such sort as best suited
with her very tender age. At that moment
I say most truly that the spirit of life which
hath its dwelling in the secretest chambers of
the heart began to beat so violently, that the
least pulses of my body shook therewith ; and
in trembling it said these words : *Ecce deus
fortior me, qui veniens dominabitur mihi.*" [1]

Singular words were these for a child of
nine to speak concerning another child of
eight, but the most singular thing about them
is their perfect truth ; the whole life of one
of the most strenuous and veracious souls that
ever lived is their verification. The impres-

[1] Symonds's *Introduction to the Study of Dante*, p. 38.

sion made upon this childish mind never faded ;
it became the motive of his life. The children do not seem to have had any compan-
ionship ; Dante often watched for a sight of
Beatrice and treasured in his memory every
glimpse of her, but it was not until nine years
after their first meeting — on the street apparently, and in company with two other
ladies — that he met her again, and she gra-
ciously spoke to him. She was dressed on
this occasion in purest white, he said, and
turning toward the place where he stood she
saluted him so kindly that he seemed to himself " to behold the utmost limits of beati-
tude." This appears to have been the only
direct communication he ever had from her.
It does not appear that she was ever aware of
the feeling she had inspired in him. The
relations of young people of their class were
closely guarded, and their consent was not
often sought in matrimonial alliances. At the
age of twenty Beatrice was married to Simon
de Bardi; it is not known that Dante ever
saw her again ; four years later she died.

That was a dark day for Dante ; it seemed
to him that the light of life had gone out.
He wrote a letter about it, he tells us, to the

city fathers, beginning with the first words of
Jeremiah's Lamentations, — " How doth the
city sit solitary ! " It was a strange thing to
do : as if the passing of this young woman
of twenty-four could be a matter of public
interest. It only shows the intensity of
Dante's nature ; to him the life of the whole
city had come to a pause. After a year of
desolation " it was given to me," he says, " to
behold a very wonderful vision, wherein I
saw things which determined me to say no
more of this most blessed one until such time
as I could discourse more worthily concerning her. And to this end I labor all I can,
as she well knoweth. Wherefore if it be
His pleasure through whom is the life of all
things that my life continue with me a few
years, it is my hope that I shall write concerning her what hath not before been written of any woman. After the which may it
seem good unto Him who is the Master of
grace that my spirit should go hence to behold the glory of its lady — to wit, of that
blessed Beatrice who now joyeth continually
on his countenance, *qui est per omnia secu-
larum benedictus, Laus Deo !* " [1]

[1] Symonds's *Introduction to the Study of Dante*, p. 48.

The five years following the death of Beatrice were busy years. Dante did not sit
glooming over his bereavement; he flung
himself into the affairs of state; he fought
in some of the wars of Florence, and in the
pauses of the strife he gave himself with ardor to study. At about the age of thirty,
by the persuasion of friends, we are told, he
married Gemma Donati, a lady of rank in
Florence, with whom he lived for a few years,
and who bore him five children. That the
marriage was an unhappy one has been asserted, but little is known about it; no word
of Dante's throws any light on this relation.
That it was a marriage of convenience rather
than affection is not doubtful; if we absolve
Dante for his share in it, it must be on the
ground of possible circumstances which we do
not understand.

When Dante was twenty-eight years old,
the democracy of Florence, in one of its radical turns, decreed that no one should take
part in the government of the city who did
not belong to some industrial or commercial guild; Dante, though an aristocrat by
birth, accordingly enrolled himself in the Guild
of Physicians and Apothecaries, — the same

Guild from which the most famous family of Florence, the Medici, took their name. By this guild he was chosen one of the priores, or chief men, of the city; he seems to have been sent abroad on one or two embassies, and to have had a considerable part in the government of the city. Just then one of the worst of the family feuds was raging in Florence, the feud of the Neri and the Bianchi, — and the streets were full of brawls. Dante advised the banishment of the leaders of both parties, and the thing was done, although kindred and intimate companions of his were among the exiles. Business of state soon after called Dante to Rome, and, in his absence, the party adverse to him gaining power, he was deposed and a sentence of exile was pronounced against him and others, with a heavy fine to be paid within two months. Refusing to heed this demand, a second sentence was hurled after him, condemning him to be burned alive if ever he set foot within the jurisdiction of Florence. This rank injustice kindled in the soul of Dante a fire that never cooled; he knew that he had deserved well at the hands of the city, and that it was the madness of partisanship that had doomed him to exile ; by every means open to him he sought to secure the overthrow of the powers inimical to him, that he might return to his home, but all in vain. Years later the offer was made to the exiles that they might return, provided they would pay a heavy fine, submit to a brief imprisonment, and walk through the streets arrayed in penitential robes. Dante's answer to this insulting proposition still blazes with righteous indignation : —

" Is this, then, the glorious return of Dante Alighieri to his country after nearly three lustres of suffering and exile ? Did an innocence patent to all merit this — this the perpetual sweat and toil of study ? Far from a man, the housemate of philosophy, be so meek and earthen-hearted a humility as to allow himself to be offered up bound, like a schoolboy or a criminal ! Far from a man, the preacher of justice, to pay those who have done him wrong as for a favor ! This is not the way of returning to my country ; but if another can be found that does not derogate from the fame and honor of Dante, that will I enter on with no flagging steps. For if by none such Florence may be entered, then by me never. Can I not everywhere behold the mirror of the sun and stars, speculate on sweetest truths under any sky, without giving myself up inglorious, nay, ignominious, to the populace and the city of Florence ?   Nor shall I want for bread." [1]

Never again did Dante behold his ancestral home.   He became the acknowledged poet of Italy, but his own city spurned him.   He lived in hope that one faction or another would call him back, and he declined to receive the poet's crown anywhere else than at the font where he had received baptism, but that recompense was denied him.   His was the life of a wanderer.   He visited many of the universities in Italy and France ; there is even a tradition, not very firm, that he made his way to Oxford; all the learning of his time he devoured.   One nobleman after another took him in and gave him temporary shelter ; some of them seem to have been not only kind to him but proud of his friendship, yet it was a bitter thing to him to live the life of a dependent.   Abundant proof had he

> " how savoreth of salt
> The bread of others, and how hard a road
> The going down and up another's stairs." [2]

[1] Quote" in Lowell's *Literary Essays*, iv. 135.
[2] *Paradiso*, xvii. 68.

He died at length in Ravenna, September 14, 1321, in the fifty-sixth year of his age, and his friend, Guido Novello, buried him. In the poet's garb they robed him for the sepulchre, and the wreath of palm that he had never worn in life was laid upon his pallid brow.

Twenty-nine years later Florence voted ten golden florins to Dante's daughter Beatrice, then a nun in Ravenna; the messenger who bore the donation was the poet Boccaccio. Half a century later Florence was ready to build a tomb to the dead prophet, " and begged in vain," says Lowell, " for the metaphorical ashes of the man of whom she had threatened to make literal cinders if she could catch him alive." In 1429 she renewed her prayer, and again, in 1519, Michelangelo stood ready to erect a worthy monument, but the Pope forbade the removal of the sacred dust. It was not until the first part of the nineteenth century, more than five hundred years after Dante's death, that a memorial of him, " ugly," says Lowell, " beyond even the usual lot of such," was placed in the church of Santa Croce ; its unsightliness makes it a suitable offering from Florence to the greatest name in all her annals.

To the work of this, the first and greatest
of the "Makers of Florence," we can give
but a glance.   It seems little less than quixotic to undertake to say anything about it
within such limitations; yet one remembers
glimpses, — like that which breaks upon the
eye when the summit of the Jura over Neu-
châtel is reached, and the Alps, at sunset,
spring into the horizon, — a few swift min-
utes, whose glory can never fade.   And if one
could grasp but the outline of this work of
Dante's, something of price would be added
to his store.

There is a Latin treatise, " De Vulgari
Eloquio," in which he argues for the production of literature in the common speech of the
people.   Up to Dante's time all European literature, with insignificant exceptions, was in
Latin.   There was one advantage in this, that
scholars of all lands had access to the whole
of literature.   You could not say with Mr.
Boffin that all print was open to them, for
print was not yet; but all letters were cosmo-
politan.   They were only for scholars, however, and Dante, like Wycliffe after him,
wanted them brought within reach of the
common people.   He argued about it in

Latin, as he needs must, for those to whom
he addressed his argument would not have
read a treatise on any learned subject in any
other tongue. But he did something better
than argue about it: he did it. His own
great poems were written in Italian, and by
that single act the common speech of the
Italian people was lifted up and glorified forever. No man, perhaps, ever did for any
other language what Dante did for the Italian. " Before the time of Shakespeare," says
Mrs. Oliphant, " the well of English undefiled
had already been opened ; but Dante formed
into written speech the tongue in which,
against all precedent, he chose to tell his great
and solemn tale. . . . And, indirectly, by
forming and giving dignity to one European
language, he emancipated all. The father
of modern literature has thus an inalienable
right to take the lead in the great line of
writers who have made the countries of Chris-
tendom known to each other, and who furnish at once the clearest and the surest revelation of the races in whose hands, for the last
five hundred years, has lain all the progress
of the world."

In view of this single service, who will

venture to estimate the debt that the world owes to Dante Alighieri? We speak of liberators, but who is like unto the man that struck from learning her scholastic fetters, and set her free to walk among the common people and speak with them, each in his own tongue in which he was born. There is a reminiscence in it of the miracle of Pentecost.

Another of Dante's prose works is "De Monarchia," a learned essay in which he seeks to show that monarchy, and a universal monarchy at that, is essential to the world's peace; that wars will never cease till all peoples are brought under one sway; that this right to rule the world belongs to the head of the Holy Roman Empire; that he derived his authority directly from God and not, *pace* Hildebrand, from God through the Pope. Still he thinks that Pope and Emperor ought to dwell in peace together, the one the temporal, the other the spiritual, ruler of the earth; that they are coördinate authorities. The church must not meddle in the affairs of state nor the state in the affairs of the church. Two things he clearly saw; first, that the state is just as sacred as the church; second, that when the church becomes a centralized ecclesiasticism there must be a clean separation of its sphere from that of the state. Great truths were these, which no man of his time had seen with equal clearness.

Of the lyrics and the letters of Dante, I must not stay to speak. There remains the great trilogy, which has made his name deathless : the " Vita Nuova," the " Convito," the " Divina Commedia," — these three, of which the greatest is the last, but all of which are vitally related.

The three books are joined together by the poet's love for Beatrice Portinari, a love so ethereal, so spiritual, that it idealizes and transfigures its object, and becomes to the soul that cherishes it as a glass through which the wonder and the glory of the whole spiritual world are revealed. I have shown you how slight was the contact of the life of Dante with that of Beatrice ; she had never been to him more than a vision or a dream, but that vision he invested with all divine perfection and worshiped it. It was not merely womanhood that he revered in her, it was glorified womanhood, apotheosized womanhood, — the highest conception that a man can entertain of purity and truth and loveliness.

The " Vita Nuova " is the simple story of Dante's youthful love, told in sonnets and canzoni, with naïve little prose commentaries on each. It was written not long after her death, and before his marriage, while he was still a resident of Florence. Little incidents are recalled of days when he saw her; slight events that reminded him of her, or of what others said about her are narrated — all with frank simplicity and worshipful tenderness. It is as pure as the song of an angel, not a shade of earthly passion clouds it. I have given you the last words of it, in which he promises, if God will let him live a few more years, to " write concerning her what hath not before been written of any woman." But that he had done already in the " Vita Nuova ; " no woman on earth or in heaven was ever glorified with such reverent love.

The " Convito " or Banquet, has been the subject of much controversy. The structure is something like that of the " Vita Nuova ; " it consists of odes, with prose commentaries upon them ; but the disquisitions and digressions of this book are far more pedantic and artificial than that of the earlier book.

It appears to be a kind of *Apologia pro*

Vita Sua, a labored attempt to explain some
episodes in his own mental history, the remembrance of which disquiets him. Some of his
songs have intimated a lack of loyalty to the
memory of Beatrice; he seems to be trying
to prove that the language which some might
so interpret was not so intended; the gentle
lady whom these poems praise was no flesh
and blood Dulcinea; it was Philosophy. Of
her he admits he has become a devotee; she
has brought him consolation in his loneliness.
" I pictured her after the fashion of a gentle
lady, and I could not picture her in any attitude save of compassion. And, moved by
this image, I began to go where she was herself to be seen in verity, to wit, to the schools
of the religious orders, and to the disputa-
tions of such as do philosophize; so that in
a short season — perhaps of thirty months —
I began to feel so much of her sweetness that
the love of her banished and destroyed all
other thought. This lady was the daughter
of God, the queen of all, most noble and fair
Philosophy." [1]

When we try to follow Dante in this Apologia we find ourselves in perplexity. His

[1] *Convito,* ii. 13; 5.

explanations do not explain. The attempt to
derive from them a consistent theory of his
mental changes is attended with great difficulties. If the "Convito" had never been
written the problem would have been simpler.
One trouble is that Beatrice is allegorized;
she becomes, at length, identified in his mind
with the divine Wisdom and Purity; and between the symbol and the thing symbolized
the thought moves freely. "We have admitted," says Mr. Lowell, "that Beatrice Portinari was a real creature, but how real she
was, and whether as real to the poet's memory as to his imagination, may fairly be ques-
tioned. She shifts, as the controlling emotion or the poetic fitness of the moment
dictates, from a woman loved and lost to a
gracious exhalation of all that is fairest in
womanhood and most divine in the soul of
man, and ere the eye has defined the new
image, it has become the old one again or
another mingled of both." [1]

The fact appears to be that the "Convito"
is a failure. It attempts to explain certain
aberrations of the affections, but the attempt
breaks down and is abandoned. He feels that

[1] *Literary Essays*, iv. 206.

his disloyalty of mind and heart are not to be accounted for, but to be confessed and forsaken. The pure ideal lays its spell upon him, and he comes back to the task of revealing to men all that he knew or could learn of that divine Wisdom and Love, whose revelation to him had come through the ascended and glorified Beatrice. This is the motive of the " Divina Commedia." His own words are the best explanation of the purpose of the poem. " The aim of the whole and the individual parts is to bring those who are living in this life out of a state of misery and to guide them to a state of happiness." To show man the nature of the sin that threatens his ruin, of the retribution that pursues him, of the discipline that restores him, of the blessedness that awaits him — this is the sublime task to which he consecrates his powers.

The framework of the poem is familiar to most of us. Dante is wandering in a gloomy and tangled wood, which symbolizes this present world, and finds himself at the foot of a hill — the height of virtue — whose summit invites him; but at the beginning of the ascent a leopard, a lion, and a she-wolf — passion, pride, and avarice — infest his path and drive him backward to the valley. Here in his distress appears to him the spirit of the old Latin poet Vergil, whom Beatrice has sent to be his guide on a journey, first through Hell and then through Purgatory, at whose confines Beatrice herself will meet him and conduct him through Paradise.

Hell, according to Dante's cosmography, is a deep funnel-shaped pit, sinking into the earth not far from Jerusalem. This pit has been formed by the fall of Satan, who, when he was cast out of heaven, " was hurled," in the words of Dr. Witte, " not merely down to the earth, but deep into its bowels, even to the dead centre, the pivot of the Universe, the deepest point of all, and the farthest removed from the presence and the light of God." [1] The steep slopes of this pit are broken by concentric circles or galleries, upon which sinners of progressive grades of wickedness receive the recompense for the deeds done in the body. At the bottom of this pit is Lucifer himself, frozen fast in solid ice, — which is not the conventional theory of his environment. Beyond this centre a narrow shaft extends to the surface of the earth on the other

---

[1] *Essays on Dante*, p. 104.

side, and near the exit thereof rises the cone-shaped Mount of Purgatory, whose convex corresponds to the concave of Hell; the one was heaped up by the same force that hollowed out the other. Round this mountain run terraces connected by stairways up which are toilfully climbing those who need to be purified by discipline before they are admitted to the life of the blessed. On its summit is the Terrestrial Paradise, from which souls ascend to the Celestial Paradise.

The abode of the blessed is fashioned in Dante's dream after the conceptions of the Ptolemaic astronomy, as nine concentric spheres; the first seven were presided over by the sun, the moon, and the five planets then known, the eighth was the heaven of the fixed stars, the ninth the Primum Mobile, the crystalline fountain of all energy and movement, which revolves from east to west once in twenty-four hours and carries all the interior spheres round with it; above and encompassing all is the Empyrean, the dwelling-place of the Eternal Light, uncreated, boundless, motionless, where elect spirits enjoy the beatific vision and are satisfied.

The structural formalism of this poem seems

at first almost a childish device. Each part contains thirty-three cantos, representing the thirty-three years of Christ's life on the earth; and in the *terza rima*, in which the whole poem is written, we are supposed to find a recognition of the Trinity. The genius of Dante appears in transcending these symbolic limitations, and in filling such artificial forms with abounding life.

What Dante sees in this eventful journey is the natural reaction of conduct upon the character. His "Inferno" is a great sermon upon the text, "Whatsoever a man soweth that shall he also reap." The greatest idealist of all literature is Dante, yet his poem is in one way tremendously realistic. An engineer could almost construct the Pit from his specifications. The figures that he brings before our eyes, any modern illustrator could easily reproduce, as Doré has done. The physical environment of these doomed souls is pictured with horrible distinctness. But the facts, after all, with which we are dealing, are the facts of the inner life; the environment has not made these people, it is they who have made the environment. Every one of them can say, and does say, in every touch of description by which he is brought before us, " Myself am hell." " The City of Dreadful Night" which he paints for us, is the dark abode which evil minds and perverse wills have created for themselves. It is no mere arbitrary infliction of sufferings, it is the logical outcome of their own conduct.

We must not, indeed, expect to find the ethical judgments of Dante infallible. He was a child of the thirteenth century, and his mind moved in the twilight of that mediævalism. It shocks us to find him consenting to the eternal exclusion from God's presence of those noble spirits whom he describes with such eloquence, and whom he found in the Limbo near the entrance of the Dolorous City: " Here there was no plaint that could be heard, except of sighs which caused the eternal air to tremble. And this arose from the sadness, without torment, of the crowds that were many and great both of children and of women and men." [1] And Vergil, his guide, who is himself a denizen of this first circle, explains the condition of its inhabitants: " Thou askest not what spirits are these thou seest ? I wish thee to know before thou goest farther that they

[1] Carlyle's *Inferno*, Canto iv.

sinned not.   And though they have merit, it
suffices not ; for they had not Baptism, which
is the portal of the faith that thou believest.
And seeing they were before Christianity,
they worshiped not God aright.   And of
these am I myself.   For such defects, and for
no other fault are we lost; and only in so
far afflicted that without hope we live on in
desire." [1]

Dante wishes to know whether any of the
good have ever been led forth from this confine-
ment, and Vergil tells him of the descent into
Hell of Christ, after his crucifixion, and of his
bearing away with him to the abode of the
blessed, Adam and Abel and Noah and Abra-
ham and Moses and David and others many:
" and I would have you know," he says, " that,
before these, human spirits were not saved."
It is evident that Dante is sorry for this un-
numbered throng of noble men and women and
of innocent unbaptized children, forever shut
out of Paradise for no fault of their own, whose
sighs make the eternal air to tremble; but there
is not a sign of moral revulsion at their hapless
fate : this is the doctrine of mother church,
and he accepts it without a qualm.

[1] Carlyle's *Inferno*, Canto iv.

Nor can we always recognize the accuracy of Dante's moral perspective in judging sins. We cannot quite understand why heretics who denied the immortality of the soul should be plunged into a lower hell than the avaricious and the incontinent, nor why suicides should be punished more condignly than murderers. On the whole, however, the insight is wonderfully true.

A grim humor gleams out now and then, as when he finds outside the gates of Hell a miserable throng of the pusillanimous — "those who lived without infamy and without praise. Mingled are they with the angels who were not rebels nor were faithful to God, but were for themselves. The heavens chased them out in order to be not less beautiful, nor doth the depth of Hell receive them, because the damned would have some glory from them." [1] Dante, like Browning and Kipling, and every apostle of the strenuous life, hates the sin of " the unlit lamp and the ungirt loin."

As we descend with him through the circles of this dismal abyss, we marvel with him at the scenery and the surroundings of these victims of their own misdoing.

[1] Norton's *Hell*, p. 12.

  " I came unto a place mute of all light,
   Which billows as the sea does in a tempest,
   If by opposing winds 't is combated.
  The infernal hurricane that never rests
   Hurtles the spirits onward in its rapine;
   Whirling them round, and smiting, it molests them.
  When they arrive before the precipice,
   There are the shrieks, the plaints, and the laments,
   There they blaspheme the puissance divine.
  I understood that unto such a torment
   The carnal malefactors were condemned,
   Who reason subjugate to appetite.
  And, as the wings of starlings bear them on
   In the cold season in large band and full,
   So doth that blast the spirits maledict;
  It hither, thither, downward, upward drives them;
   No hope doth comfort them forevermore,
   Not of repose, but even of lesser pain." [1]

What a vision is this of the eternal unrest
which a life of incontinence engenders! And
here is a picture of the avaricious : —

  " E'en as a billow on Charybdis rising,
   Against encountered billow dashing breaks,
   Such is the dance this wretched race must lead,
  Whom more than elsewhere numerous here I found;
  From one side and the other, with loud voice,
   Both roll'd on weights by main force of their breasts,
  Then smote together, and each one forthwith
  Roll'd them back voluble, turning again,
  Exclaiming, these, ' Why holdest thou so fast ? '
  These answering, ' And why castest thou away? '
  So still repeating their despiteful song,
  They to the opposite point on either hand

    [1] Longfellow's *Inferno*, v. 28–45.

Travers'd the horrid circle; there arrived,
Both turn'd them round, and through the middle space
Conflicting met again." [1]

This is what we sometimes describe on earth as competition. Dante's idea is that those who devote their lives to it here may expect to go on with it forever; that it becomes an irresistible habit, the nightmare of eternity.

The sullen and the melancholy are plunged in putrid mud: "There are people underneath the water who sob and make it bubble at the surface as thy eye may tell thee, whichever way it turns. Fixed in the slime they say: Sullen were we in the sweet air that is gladdened by the sun, carrying lazy smoke within our hearts; now lie we here sullen in the black mire. This hymn they gurgle in their throats, for they cannot speak it in full words." [2]

The suicides, who despised their bodies, inhabit trees; usurers have lost their identity and masquerade as money-bags. "The flatterers," says Dr. Harris, condensing many pages of this narrative, "wallow in filth. They are engaged in destroying the rational self-

[1] Cary's *Inferno*, vii. 22–36.
[2] Carlyle's *Inferno*, vii. 117–126.

estimate of those whom they flatter by calling evil good and good evil, and producing a
confusion between clean and unclean. The
Simonists buy and sell the offices of the church
for money, and are plunged, likewise, head first
into round holes or purses while flames scorch
the soles of their feet. As others follow them
they sink toward the bottom of the earth,
gravitating toward pelf. Their deeds directly
destroy the spiritual by making it subservient
to money and material gain; they invert the
true order of the spiritual and material and
symbolically place the head where the feet
should be." [1]

Dante finds one of the popes who had sold
bishoprics and offices for money in this in-
verted posture, with flames licking the soles
of his feet; he seems to be gratified at coming upon him there, and administers to him
a roasting not much gentler than that of the
sulphurous flame : —

> "I pray thee tell me now how great a treasure
> Our Lord demanded of St. Peter, first,
> Before he put the keys into his keeping.
> Truly he nothing asked but 'follow me.'
> Nor Peter nor the rest asked of Matthias
> Silver or gold, when he by lot was chosen

[1] *The Spiritual Sense of Dante's Divina Commedia*, p. 68.

Unto the place the guilty soul had lost.
Therefore stay here, for thou art justly punished,
And keep safe guard o'er the ill-gotten money." [1]

Dante was a good Churchman, but he was not, I dare say, a believer in papal infallibility, for he finds several popes in Hell, and brings back word that the pope even then reigning was daily expected to arrive there.

The diviners, soothsayers, and astrologists, who make a trade of an assumed knowledge of the future, are pictured as " wondrously distorted, from the chin to the commencement of the chest," so that the face was turned toward the loins, and they had to come backward, for to look before them was denied. On which let us hear Dr. Harris's subtle comment : —

" One who knows the future knows it as already happened, and hence turns all events into something that has already happened, that is to say, into a past. For him there is no present or future ; all is past time. Hence the meaning of the punishment, by twisting the head around so as to look backward. They look at all as past, instead of standing like rational beings between the past and the fu-

[1] Longfellow's *Inferno*, xix. 90-98.

ture, and on the basis of the accomplished facts of the past, building new possibilities into facts by the exercise of their wills." [1]

I can dwell no longer on this symbolism. The grim scenery of Hell I have not sought to reproduce for you; you may go to Doré for that. It is rather the substance of Hell as Dante conceives it — the inevitable consequences of evil doing — that I have cared to dwell upon. All is symbolic, of course; but the reality here symbolized is as stern and sure a reality as human reason can contemplate.

One thing we may remark before we pass from the " Inferno," — the clear judgment of the poet in representing sins that undermine society as worse than sins which degrade the individual. The men who used public trusts corruptly, the men who sold office or official power for money, the men who had betrayed for gain the city or the state, Dante thrusts into the deepest Hell; he ranks them as worse than drunkards and debauchees, or even than the murderers. " In the fifth ditch," says Dr. Harris, " are punished the sinners who sell public offices for money. They sell justice, too, for money; [and they would, of course,

---

[1] *The Spiritual Sense of Dante's Divina Commedia*, p. 69.

have sold franchises and contracts for money
if they had had any to sell] thus confusing all
moral order. They are plunged in boiling
pitch and tormented by demons with long
forks. Dante is actually diverted at the punishment of these mischief-makers, with whom
he has become so well acquainted through the
politics of his time." [1]

Dante's moral perspective is perfectly accurate at this point. If there is any class of
malefactors whose misdeeds deserve torments
most dire, it is these who thus make public
office a source of private gain. They are doing what they can to make society impossible,
and to bring hell to earth. It would be an
immense benefit to the world if they could all
be sent straight to the place which Dante has
provided for them.

In passing with Dante and Vergil from the
dismal Pit to the hopeful Mountain we experience a great sense of relief. The second
book of the Commedia is far less known than
the first, but it is better worth knowing. Its
scenery is less weird, its symbolisms less grotesque, but its insight is no less true. For all

[1] *Spiritual Sense*, pp. 69, 70.

these souls in Purgatory there is hope. They are suffering, but it is good discipline; they are all looking forward to deliverance. There is no bitterness here, but good-will and helpfulness; the soul is at one with God and with its kind. This is a steep and rugged mountain, up whose spiral terraces they are climbing, but the higher they go the easier is the ascent.

The disciplinary sufferings which Dante has provided for these various classes of penitents are not less suggestive than his reports of penalties in the "Inferno." The angel who keeps the gate of Purgatory inscribes on the forehead of each who enters seven *P's* — *peccata* — representing the seven deadly sins which are to be purged away in the ascent. As the penitent goes up from one terrace to another, having been cleansed from the sin of which the lower circle was the place of discipline, he hears a sound of music, one of the seven stigmata drops from his forehead, and his load is lightened, so that the ascent is easier.

On the lowest terrace souls are cleansed from pride. Heavy weights are given them to carry, which bend them to the earth. On the mountain wall of the terrace are carved in white marble beautiful representations of true humility, and in the pavement over which they must go with downcast faces are sculptured scenes from history which tell of the wars that pride entails. Thus they are chastened for their pride in body and mind.

The next terrace is the purge of envy; and the penitents have their eyelids sewn together with iron wire, because their sin was one that made them blind to the good in their fellowmen. For them there are no sculptured scenes to admonish them of their fault and draw them to virtue, but voices in the air are heard praising generous deeds and rehearsing the miseries of those who have been the prey of envious passion.

On the third ledge the wrathful are disciplined; the slothful on the fourth, the avaricious on the fifth, the gluttonous and the intemperate on the sixth, the lustful on the seventh; thence through a baptism of fire the soul ascends to the earthly Paradise.

On all this journey there is high discourse between Dante and Vergil, and sweet morsels of conversation with the ascending souls; many of the deep things of philosophy, many

of the vital truths of conduct, many of the
burning questions of social and political science occupy their thoughts. One willingly
lingers on the mount of purification, where
the scenery is often so beautiful, —

> " Gold and fine silver, ceruse, cochineal,
>   India's rich wood, heaven's lucid blue serene,
> Or glow that emeralds freshly broke reveal,
>   Had all been vanquished by the varied sheen
> Of this bright valley, set with shrubs and flowers,
>   As less by greater ; "

where the twilights are so lovely :

> " 'T was now the hour that brings to men at sea
>   Who in the morn have bid sweet friends farewell,
> Fond thoughts and longing with them back to be,
>   And thrills the pilgrim with a tender spell
> Of love, if haply, new upon his way,
>   He faintly hears a chime from some far bell
> That seems to mourn the dying of the day ; " [1]

where morning comes with such a tender grace :

> " Just at the hour when her sad lay begins
>   The little swallow, near unto the morning,
>   Perchance in memory of her former woes,
> And when the mind of man, a wanderer
>   More from the flesh and less by thought imprisoned,
>   Almost prophetic in its visions is ; " [2]

where, amidst sore pains and under galling
burdens there is so much of human friendship ;

[1] Parsons's *Purgatorio*, vii., viii.
[2] Longfellow's *Purgatorio*, ix. 13–18.

and where the mountain itself trembles with joy and the *Gloria in Excelsis* breaks forth whenever a penitent finishes one stage of his discipline and goes upward purified to freer and larger life.

One vital element the Christian of to-day misses in all this discipline. There is no suggestion of the personal friendship of Christ in the experience of these penitents. They are not comforted and encouraged by communion with Him. He is not here. He is far away in that world of light to which they are climbing. He has done his work once for all; He has made his sacrifice for them, and they have availed themselves of it, sacramentally; but they never think of Him as walking with them by the way and sharing with them their conflicts and their victories. It is a strange defect of the interpretation.

The spirit of Jesus is here, in the lives of the penitents, in their sympathy with one another, in their prayers for those who are coming after them; but that sense of his presence, that comradeship with Him which has been so deep an experience in the lives of all the great saints, Catholic and Protestant, from Saint Paul and Saint Bernard to Phillips

Brooks, Dante does not find in his study of the souls upon the upward way.

At the entrance of the earthly Paradise Vergil resigns his charge, and Dante, under the guidance of the fair Matilda, who represents virtue in action, beholds an apocalyptic vision of the triumph of Christ and his church. Then, out of the highest heaven, descends to him the glorified Beatrice of his life's dream to lead him through the shining pathway of Paradise to the Beatific Vision : —

> " Ere now have I beheld, as day began,
>   The eastern hemisphere, all tinged with rose,
> And the other heaven, with fair serene adorned,
>   And the sun's face, uprising, overshadowed,
>   So that by tempering influence of vapors
>   For a long interval the eye sustained it ;
> Thus, from the bosom of a cloud of flowers
>   Which from those hands angelical ascended,
>   And downward fell again inside and out
> Over her snow-white veil with olive cinct,
>   Appeared a lady under a green mantle,
>   Vested in color of the living flame."

By the awe and the thrill which as a child he had felt in her presence, once more his whole soul is shaken, and deeper even than this is the sense of shame for his own misdeeds with which the sight of her heavenly purity overwhelms him.   There is humble confession and

forgiveness; the waters of Lethe wash away
the memory of the evil of his life and the
waters of Eunoe revive the remembrance of
life's good; thus is he cleansed and fitted for
the flight through Paradise.

On that great journey we cannot now follow him. Let Mr. Symonds give you, in a few
swift sentences, the spirit of this vision: —

" Throughout these regions hope is swallowed in fruition, prayer is lost in praise. By
heavenly alchemy the woes of earth are turned
to gladness, and the whole world in the light
of God seems beautiful. . . . The souls dis-
play their happiness by increase of radiance.
' From joy in heaven splendor grows like smiles
on earth.' Here light and love and joy are
one, a triune element in which the spirits dance
and sing. . . . Melody and movement are the
life of Paradise as light its element and love
its joy, and as its science is the sight of God's
unclouded lustre. . . . The state of the saints
is one of boundless love. There is no jealousy
and no disparity in heaven. When a stranger
comes they cry, ' See one who will increase
our love.'

" It is a strange world, this Paradise conceived by Dante, unlike anything that earlier

poet dreamed or ever saw in trance revealed to him. . . . None but the purest soul could have rejoiced to bathe itself in that illimitable sea of love. The 'endless morn of light' which Milton dreamed of Dante realized. His spirit 'shaping wings' for the eternal shore, in exile, age, and disappointment, sang these deathless songs of joy — so high, so piercing, that the ear scarcely sustains their intense melody.

"To appreciate the "Paradiso" rightly, we require a portion of Shelley's or Beethoven's soul. It is only some 'unbodied joy,' some spirit rapt by love above the vapors and the sounds of earth that dares to soar or can breathe long in this ethereal rare atmosphere. . . . What a man brings to Dante's poem he will find there. Those to whom music, light, and love are elemental as the air they breathe will be at home in Paradise." [1]

Here we must part with our light-bearer. Miss Rossetti's fine interpretation is called "The Shadow of Dante;" less than that I have shown you; it is but the thinnest wraith of him that you have seen to-night. If I could have had seven evenings instead of one I

[1] *Introduction to the Study of Dante*, pp. 184, 185.

might have helped you to see Dante Alighieri, to hear him, perhaps to love him. We must content ourselves with this glimpse of the father of modern literature, the fiery champion of freedom and justice, the clear witness to the great verities revealed in the Incarnation of the Christ, the exile and the wanderer, who, for his fidelity to truth, was banished from his home and forced to eat the bitter bread of poverty; the strong-faced man, with aquiline profile and hollow cheeks and eyes, with fire glowing in their depths, whose words were few save when his soul was stirred, and to whom the children pointed as they saw his gaunt figure and his downcast visage upon the street, saying, "Hush! he has been in hell!" — above all, the great prophet and interpreter of human life, who has bound the present and the future together with indissoluble bonds, and has shown us, through the shadows which his imagination has evoked, so much of the substance of both hell and heaven.

Michelangelo, who was born a century and a half after Dante's death, knew the Commedia almost by heart, and filled the margins of his sumptuous copy with annotations and pen-

cil-sketches of its scenes. With Michelangelo's
sonnet upon Dante our study may fitly close: —

" No tongue can tell of him what should be told,
    For on blind eyes his splendor shines too strong ;
    'T were easier to blame those who wrought him wrong,
    Than sound his least praise with a mouth of gold.
He, to explore the place of pain was bold,
    Then soared to God, to teach our souls by song ;
    The gates heaven oped to bear his feet along,
    Against his just desire his country rolled.
Thankless I call her, and to her own pain
    The nurse of fell mischance ; for sign take this,
    That ever to the best she deals more scorn :
Among a thousand proofs, let one remain :
    Though ne'er was fortune more unjust than his,
    His equal or his better ne'er was born." [1]

---

[1] *The Sonnets of Michelangelo,* Translated by John Addington Symonds, II.

II

MICHELANGELO, THE ARTIST

Rude and unpleasing as they may sometimes be, his figures are never petty nor ordinary. In these bold forms, grandly outlined, and executed with unsurpassable breadth and freedom, he sets before us a higher type of being, in whose presence everything low falls from us, and our feelings experience the same elevation that they do before true tragedy. Lastly, that which ever and anew sympathetically attracts us, even to those of his figures which we at first found repellent, is the fact that they are inwardly allied to the best within us, to our own striving after all that is high and ideal. — *Wilhelm Lübke.*

No one, not even the dullest, not the weakest, not the laziest and lustfullest, not the most indifferent to ideas, or the most tolerant of platitudes and paradoxes, can pass him by without being arrested, quickened, stung, purged, stirred to uneasy self-examination by so strange a personality, expressed in prophecies of art so pungent. — *John Addington Symonds.*

He divorced himself from the Renaissance to join with the great Christian school of a preceding time. He is great because in the vaulting of the Sistine Chapel he recreated the prophets and the sybils and impressed them all with the nobility of his own soul. He is great, above all, through his suffering. In the presence of those strange figures of the Medici tombs we hear that cry which man would ever stop his ears against, and yet perforce must always listen to hear, — the cry of suffering of the human soul. — *Marcel Reymond.*

MICHELANGELO BUONAROTTI (ATTRIBUTED TO BUGIARDINI)

MICHELANGELO, THE ARTIST

WHEN Dante died, in 1321, his great successor Petrarch was seventeen years old. Petrarch's father was one of those White Guelfs
who had been banished from Florence with
Dante, nineteen years before. I bring these
dates together because Petrarch was the first
great figure of the Renaissance on the side of
learning and letters.

What was this Renaissance, this rebirth of
civilization in Europe ? What were the causes
which produced it and the signs by which it
was manifested ?

In the downfall of the old Roman Empire
and the triumph of Christianity, the art and
the learning of Greece and Rome practically
disappeared. For this two reasons may be
given.

The struggle between Christianity and Paganism was a fight to the death; it soon became evident that one or the other must go

down. Doubtless there were surreptitious
and unconscious compromises, and Christianity did incorporate into its life Pagan elements — some that were beneficial and some
that were baleful; but for the most part the
two systems stood in sharp antagonism, and
the life of the one meant the death of the
other. The learning and the art of Greece
and Rome were, in the minds of the early
Christians, inextricably mingled with the Pagan religion; they could not discriminate;
all went into the pit together. Just so, in a
later century, the Puritans stripped their lives
of beauty, because beauty was an essential
element of the ritual against which they re-
volted.

The other reason for the disappearance of
the classic culture was the fact that the untu-
tored people who came down from the German forests and took possession of Italy and
Rome were not at all ready to receive and ap-
propriate these treasures of art and learning.
Some centuries must pass before they would
be sufficiently civilized to enjoy the sculptures
of Phidias and Praxiteles, and the poems of
Sophocles and Horace, and the reasonings
of Plato and Cicero. While, therefore, the

germs of this ancient art and learning were never wholly destroyed, there was small chance for them, among the tangled growths of the Middle Ages, to come to full fruition.

Christianity itself — the Christianity of the church — was grievously debased and adulterated in its struggle with this mass of mediæval barbarism. The pure doctrines of the New Testament were mixed with all sorts of superstitions and absurdities. The vital elements were there, and the life would at length triumph over all these deformities and parasitic infestations, but many centuries would pass before the regeneration would be complete. During all this period one of the defects of Christianity was, no doubt, its contempt for the art and learning of the old world. That antagonism was natural and inevitable, but it was, nevertheless, injurious to Christianity.

We have, then, in the Middle Ages a triangular combat : the Pagan Culture, the Christian Faith, the Barbarian Power, each arrayed against both the others. Christianity must set itself in array against Paganism because of its idolatries and immoralities, and in so doing it separated itself from the art and

learning of the old world and greatly steril-
ized its own life.

Christianity must convert and subdue the
barbarians of the North, but, as was inevitable, it stooped to conquer, and the pure faith
was sadly alloyed with many a gross admix-
ture of superstition. But the transformation
of the tribes, though slow and painful, was
gradually accomplished, and when the peoples
were led out of the wilderness they were ready
for the reviving touch upon their lives of the
ancient art and learning. Christianity, freed
from the deadly grasp of Paganism, had subdued European barbarism, and was now waiting to be reconciled, on such terms as it could
make, with what was best in the ancient culture.

The crusades made ready for this recon-
ciliation, for the returning crusaders brought
back from the East reports of a civilization
more advanced than that of Europe ; and the
capture of Constantinople by the Turks in
1453 scattered the Greek scholars and their
books all over Europe, and gave an immense
impulse to the study of the ancient literature.

The beginning of the Renaissance, or Re-

vival of Learning, is, then, difficult to fix.   Petrarch is, as I have said, generally counted as
its first great name ; yet you do not forget
that Dante was full of the ancient learning ;
that Vergil was his guide through the lower
regions ; that he mingles the demigods and
heroes of the old mythology promiscuously
with Hebrew prophets and saints in the
trenches of the Pit and on the terraces of
Purgatory, and that his enthusiasm for the
ancient literature is always breaking forth in
his song.   Still, it must be said that Dante,
in his conceptions of life, was essentially mediæval, while Petrarch had imbibed the spirit
of the Greek culture.   In his poetry, as in
the tales of Boccaccio, there was but little of
the allegorical and the mystical ; we have a
simpler style, and a more direct look upon
nature.   From this day forward the influence
of the Greek learning and art steadily grows.
In Italy this movement had its rise, and its
greatest gains were here harvested.   The
Latin classics, a long-despised inheritance,
were recovered, and studied with passionate
devotion.   Old manuscripts were sought out
and edited and printed ; libraries of them
were collected ; princes devoted their revenues

to the new learning. Nor did their zeal exhaust itself in the rehabilitation of Latinity; the Greek language was also resurrected, and the Attic philosophers and poets were read in their own tongue with wondering delight.

The impulse traveled north from Italy, and the effect of it upon the life of Europe was marvelous. For now that the old learning had come back and its conceptions had begun to mingle in men's minds with the Christian ideals, it was evident at once that there were still radical differences between them. The touch of the new learning upon the old life was like the Prince's kiss upon the lips of the Sleeping Beauty, but there were armed men in the retinue thus roused who had a right to challenge the authority of the newcomer. That the beauty of nature is worthy of our admiration, and that the natural joys of life are not to be despised, was the truth that the recovered culture brought back to men's thought; but there was great danger that, in the eagerness with which they welcomed this message, the deeper truth, that spiritual perfection is the supreme thing, and that we attain unto this only through struggle and conflict, would be neglected or forgotten.

Through the whole period of the Renaissance
the spirit of the Pagan culture, which makes
the love of natural beauty supreme, was contending for the mastery with the spirit of
Christianity, which exalts and crowns the spiritual nature. To unite the two and give each
its proper place was the problem, and it was
not to be solved without toil and strife.
The precious elements in the Pagan culture
must be regained, but they must not be al-
lowed to extinguish the more precious elements
which Christianity had developed.

A recent writer tells us that the culminat-
ing point of the Renaissance, the moment of
the greatest activity of this movement for the
restoration of the old learning and art, was
reached about 1475. That was the year
that Michelangelo was born. Michelangelo
Buonarotti Simoni is the sonorous Italian
name which he carried through life. His father was a native of Florence, one of the lesser
nobles of that illustrious city, poor as a church
mouse, and of course disabled by the fact of
his aristocratic birth from productive industry,
though not from that species of mendicancy
which is the sole occupation of decayed aris-
tocrats. Ludovico di Leonardo Buonarotti

Simoni had been appointed, in 1474, podesta or chief magistrate of the little town of Caprese in the Caventine, among the hills, southeast of Florence, and it was here that Michelangelo was born, March 6, 1475.

The term of his father's magistracy was brief, only part of a year, and the family soon returned to Florence. In Settïgnano, a rustic suburb of that city, the Buonarotti possessed a small farm, and the infant was put out to nurse in the home of one of the tenants. The foster-mother was the wife of a stone-cutter, and the sculptor used to say, in later years, that his love of the chisel and the mallet was drawn in with his nurse's milk. When he was of school age a grammarian of Florence named Francesco de Urbino had the first training of him, but in that school he was a dull pupil; chalk or pencil was always in his hand; the bent of his genius even now was irresistible. A certain youth named Granacci, then in the studio of the brothers known as Ghirlandajo, was his friend; from him he used to get prints, drawings, and sketches of various sorts, of which he made copies of astonishing accuracy. Nor was he a mere imitator. Whenever he got a copper-plate he wanted to reproduce it in color, and if he could borrow paints and brushes, he would astonish the artists by the freedom and mastery of his treatment. His father fought against his penchant, and did his best to scourge it out of him, but it was unavailing; his spirit knew its high calling and election of God and was bound to make it sure. Before long he had mastered his father's scruples and was apprenticed to Ghirlandajo for three years; for compensation he was to receive six florins the first year, eight the second, and ten the third, the entire wages of the three years equaling a little more than forty dollars in our money. At once his masterful faculty asserted itself. How much he learned of his teachers is not known; very little, perhaps. But he was surrounded by works of art, and he had eyes of his own, and an imagination. It was not, I suppose, any easier for an ordinary man to teach Michelangelo to draw than for an ordinary mathematician to teach Isaac Newton the proper solution of an algebraic problem. Just as the boy Newton saw through the whole operation at a glance, long before the teacher could even state it, so the young Florentine by an

artistic intuition caught with a look the exact
relation of forms and colors, of lights and
shades, and the picture or the statue was before his mind's eye with absolute definiteness.
Learning to draw is mainly learning to see,
and that was a lesson Michelangelo learned
before he began to make pictures. Indeed he
seems to have been a veritable genius; his faculties needed not the kind of schooling which
most of us require.

Michelangelo was supposed to be learning
to paint in the studio of Ghirlandajo, but
some one gave him a piece of refuse marble
and he borrowed a chisel and mallet and
struck out of it the head of a grinning Faun,
which is shown to-day in Florence. His first
work in marble is a work of art.

Naturally such a pupil was not likely to be
in high favor with his master, for Michelangelo was not at all unconscious of his own
power, and he doubtless knew that no one in
that workshop could teach him anything. A
story is told of his finding on the easel a
drawing, by his master, of a female figure,
and of his taking the pencil and boldly cor-
recting the outline, making it visibly truer to
life. Vasari had the original drawing as a

keepsake, and he says of it : " Wonder it was
to see the difference of the two styles and to
note the judgment and ability of a mere boy,
so spirited and bold, who had the courage to
chastise his master's handiwork." [1] Such episodes did not conduce to harmony in the studio of Ghirlandajo. Haydn and Beethoven,
in later years, repeated this incompatibility of
great master and greater pupil. The hen is
a useful fowl, but she is not a good nursing
mother for the eagle.

This apprenticeship, for such reasons as
these, was not to be completed ; after a year
with Ghirlandajo there came a request from
Lorenzo the Magnificent for two promising
pupils to reside with him and study in the
Medicean gardens of sculpture, and the master, perhaps with some sense of relief, recom-
mended Michelangelo and his friend Granacci.

It was not easy to secure the consent of
Ludovico Buonarotti to the removal of his
son to the service of Lorenzo. The seedy old
aristocrat had a notion that they were going
to make a stone-cutter of the boy ; Granacci
was obliged to reason long with him to prove
that the occupation of a sculptor was not

[1] Quoted by Symonds, *Life of Michelangelo*, i. 17.

beneath his son's rank. But when Ludovico was summoned into the presence of the Magnificent his scruples were overcome by the offer of a job for himself in the Custom House, and the youth was taken under the patronage of Lorenzo, in whose palace, from the beginning of his fifteenth to the beginning of his eighteenth year, he had his home.

It is doubtful whether any other place in the world, in that day or any other, could have offered him an environment so full of stimulus to his intellect and taste. Lorenzo de Medici was himself the central figure of the Italian Renaissance. It is not necessary to estimate his character, but he was a great diplomatist, and politician, a great patron of art and letters, and a man of no mean accomplishments as poet and critic.

The Casa Medici was itself a great art museum. It was crowded with statues in bronze and marble by the best of modern sculptors, its walls were hung with paintings by the great contemporary artists; collectors from all the East had gathered to its store vases, intaglios, coins, every kind of artistic product. In a library, which was the marvel of the age, were assembled not only the choicest printed books but the rarest and most precious manuscripts.

To this honey were drawn the bees of every clime. Scholars, philosophers, poets, artists, were welcomed by the Magnificent, not as guests merely, but as inmates of his home; his table was constantly surrounded by the intellectual leaders of civilization. Marsilio Ficino, renowned as an interpreter of Plato; Pico della Mirandola, the marvelous Orientalist; Politian, professor and poet; Pulci, the humorist, with a great array of names less illustrious, were dwellers beneath this roof, all of them engaged in the studies congenial to themselves, and sharing with one another the spoils of their common enterprise. " Rarely," says Symonds, " at any period of the world's history, perhaps only in Athens between the Persian and the Peloponnesian wars, has culture, in the highest and best sense of that word, prospered more than it did in the Florence of Lorenzo, through the coöperation and mutual zeal of men of eminence, inspired by common enthusiasms, and laboring in diverse though cognate fields of study and production." [1]

[1] *Life of Michelangelo,* i. 25.

Despite the apprehensions of Ludovico Buonarotti, the place of Michelangelo in this
home was not that of a menial. He was but
a youth, but he was a youth of genius, and
the recognition which was due to him was not
withheld. He was dressed as one to the manner born; his apartment in the palace was
a comfortable one; he had the pocket money
without which a boy's life is somewhat clouded;
in all respects his position was that of a son
and not that of a servant. The democracy of
culture gave the laws to the table of the Magnificent; guests took their seats, not according to their rank, but in the order of their
arrival, so that Michelangelo might be seated
any day near the head of the table, and in
the midst of the great scholars and artists
who filled the house, and who were already so
much impressed with his great abilities that
they freely conversed with him and encouraged him in his high purposes. In this, it
is evident, they were reflecting the judgment
of the master of the house, who was wont to
send often for Michelangelo, to consult him
regarding the merits of the rare objects of art
which he was then collecting.

Thus we find the young artist launched

upon his career under most prosperous skies, all the winds and all the tides conspiring to set him forward. He was yet to have dark days and rough seas enough, but his youth was one of the fairest fortune. The small office which Lorenzo had given his father provided for the wants of his family; the undivided attention of the boy could be given to the study and the practice of the art to which his life was devoted.

It might be well to pause here and glance about us at what is going on in the world while Michelangelo is pursuing his studies in the Medicean gardens. It is from 1489 to 1492 that this felicity continues. Looking back we remember that Dante had now been in his grave one hundred and seventy years, and Petrarch, his successor, more than a century; the seventh Henry is upon the English throne; the reckless and audacious Charles VIII. is reigning in France; the Pope is Innocent VIII., the least innocent of all the Innocents, perhaps, and that is a strong saying; the Emperor is the parsimonious and pusillanimous Frederick III. Thirty-nine years have passed since the dispersion of the scholars by the fall of Constantinople; by this time, like the persecuted apostles, they have gone everywhere, preaching the word. Thirty-eight years only have elapsed since the first book was printed with movable types, yet it is marvelous how rapidly, during that time, the number of printed books has increased, and how beautifully they are printed ; that famous Venetian press of Aldo Manuzio, whose issues are so prized by book-lovers in these days, and whose pages are so admired by modern book-makers, had just been set in operation. The Ptolemaic astronomy is still producing vertigo in thinkers' heads, with its eccentrics and epicycles and primum mobile, but its doom is sealed ; the Prussian boy Copernicus is now, in his eighteenth year, studying medicine at Padua ; he will prescribe, presently, for that malady. There is no western continent that men of the east have yet seen, but there is a far Cathay of which they have dreamed, and Columbus, during these very years of Angelo's residence in the Medicean palace, is getting his fleet together, and will sail, in the last of these years, in search of lands beyond the sea. Are not these eventful times ? The whole horizon is ablaze with light.

Of the artists of Italy some of the great

names are already written on tombs; Brunel-
leschi, who lifted in air the great dome of
Florence, has been dead almost half a century; and Ghiberti, whose gates in front of
the Florentine baptistery were fit, as Angelo
said, for the portal of Paradise, a little longer.
Fra Angelico has been with the angels that
he loved for nearly two score years, and Lippo
Lippi for more than a score; Andrea del
Sarto is a child of five years old, Raphael is
a lad of nine, Titian a boy of twelve, and
Leonardo da Vinci a man of forty; the world
must still wait two years for the arrival in
the flesh of the spirit of Correggio, and four
for Benvenuto Cellini. In the realm of art it
will be seen that between the young immortals and the young mortals great work has
already been done, and greater is still to come.

Among the influences which were helping
to shape the character of the young Michelangelo during these years in the palace of
Lorenzo none, perhaps, was deeper or more
decisive than that of the mighty monk Savonarola, whose preaching in the great Duomo
was shaking Florence as it had never before
been shaken. In the very year in which the
boy was summoned by Lorenzo to the palace,

the preacher was called by the same potentate
to return to Florence. He had preached there
before, to few and listless hearers; but a baptism of fire had fallen on him in Lombardy,
and now the city could not choose but hear
him. No more trenchant preaching was ever
heard; the luxury and frivolity of Florence
were rebuked with the most terrific invective; the tyranny of rulers, the corruption of
politics, the heartlessness and oppression of
the rich, were judged unsparingly, and the
doom of the eternal judgment was threatened
against these sinners if they did not speedily
repent.

" Michelangelo," says his biographer, " was
one of his constant listeners at St. Marco
and the Duomo. He witnessed those stormy
scenes of religious revival and passionate fa-
naticism which contemporaries have impres-
sively described. The shorthand writer to
whom we owe the text of Savonarola's sermons at times breaks off with words like
these: ' Here I was so overcome with weeping that I could not go on.' Pico della Mirandola tells us that the mere sound of the
monk's voice, startling the voice of the Duomo,
thronged through all its space with people,

was like a clap of doom; a cold shiver ran
through the marrow of his bones, the hairs
of his head stood on end while he listened.
Another witness reports: 'The sermons caused
such terror, alarm, sobbing and tears, that
every one passed through the streets without
speaking, more dead than alive.' " [1]

Imagine the impression made upon the
mind of a youth as sensitive and serious as
Michelangelo by such intense and terrible
moral earnestness as that of Savonarola. We
do not wonder that through all his life he
treasured the memory of the great monk,
with whose desires for the reformation of the
church and the freedom of Florence he so
heartily sympathized, nor that, in later years,
his Savonarola and his Bible were studied
together. Symonds is warranted in his con-
jecture that " the apocalyptical thunderings
and voices of the Sistine Chapel owe much
of their soul-thrilling impressiveness to those
studies," and Michelet in declaring that " the
spirit of Savonarola lives again in the frescoes
of that vault." [2]

Thus we behold the education of the youth

---

[1] Symonds's *Life of Michelangelo,* i. 37.
[2] *Ibid.* p. 38.

proceeding under influences of an altogether
exceptional character. In the home of Lorenzo the Magnificent, for three years, with
the noonday splendors of the Renaissance
blazing around him, with such opportunities
of personal contact with the most vigorous
and influential minds of his age as few young
men have enjoyed, he certainly was enabled
to know and to feel the full force of that
mighty intellectual movement by which the
ancient culture returned to take possession of
the soul of man.   And yet he was first and
last and always a Christian ; the central ideas
of the Christian religion never lost their
power over his mind, and under the fiery tui-
tion of Savonarola they were indelibly burned
into his experience. Is it not clear that the
two forces which we have found contending
for the mastery in the world about him have
both got possession of his soul ; that his own
consciousness is sure to be the arena of a
momentous struggle ; that the work of his
life will be full of the signs of storm and
stress.

In 1492 his great patron died and the hal-
cyon days were at an end.   Lorenzo's son
Piero was a trifler ; soon came the revolution

and swept him from power. Michelangelo betook himself to Bologna, and there, for a year, he studied Dante and practiced his art, producing some good work; some time in 1495 he returned to Florence. The city was now practically under the power of Savonarola; a Puritanic seriousness and simplicity had replaced the luxurious revels of the later Mediceans, and Michelangelo had for a few months a quiet breathing spell, in which he was able to meditate some excellent work. He was now twenty-one years of age, and already his chisel had produced several notable statues. One of these was a Sleeping Cherub, which was soiled to make it look like an antique (for there were tricks in all trades even in those good old times), and sold, but not by Angelo, for a large price, to a nobleman in Rome. The purchaser found out the fraud, but he also discovered the artist and brought him straight to Rome.

It is impossible for me to follow in detail the events of the life of Michelangelo from this time forward; let me give, in merest outline, first his principal movements from place to place; next a brief reference to some of his more important works, and finally some account of his personal qualities and friendships.

From this twenty-first year most of his life was spent at Rome, though he returned several times to Florence, each time executing there important works which are now among the glories of the Tuscan capital.

To his first residence in Rome we must ascribe at least three of his masterpieces, the athletic Cupid, now in the South Kensington Museum, the Pieta, in St. Peter's at Rome, and the Madonna and Child, in the Church of Notre Dame at Bruges. These must have been prosperous days with him : why his work in Rome was interrupted we do not know ; probably it was some call from that impecunious family, which was always a burden to him, that took him back to Florence after nearly four years in the Eternal City. He returned to his home with a fresh and growing fame, and found important commissions awaiting him ; the colossal David, and the only movable painting that we can confidently attribute to him, — the Holy Family in the Uffizi Gallery, — are the fruits of this sojourn of these years in Florence. The most ambitious work of that period, his cartoon of

The Bathers, has perished. In 1505 he was
called back to Rome by Pope Julius II. The
new Pope was himself a man of restless energy; he wanted to do the greatest things,
largely for his own glory; he desired to see
prodigious works of art rising about him to
illustrate and commemorate his reign, and
Michelangelo was clearly the man whose co-
operation he must secure. The relation between Pope Julius and Michelangelo was often
warlike; they were two of a kind; Angelo was
something of a pope himself, yet they continued to have a good deal of affection for
each other. They quarreled, several times,
and were reconciled; the artist once ran away
to Florence and the Pontiff long besought
him in vain to return ; after a time, the Pope
being in Bologna, Angelo compromised so far
as to go thither to see him; he would meet
the Pope halfway. When he was ushered
into the papal presence, the bishop who presented him ventured to apologize for the artist's recusancy, when the Pope turned upon
the episcopal apologist and boxed his ears
and turned him out of the room for insulting the artist; thus the breach was healed.
Julius had a great plan for a tomb for him-

self at St. Peter's ; that was the work in which
he sought to employ Michelangelo ; it was
to be a stupendous construction as Angelo
sketched it, — three stories high with multi-
tudes of marble figures, some of them colossal ; it was too big, in fact, for St. Peter's,
and therefore the old church must be torn
down and a new one begun which should be
capacious enough to make room for it. Angelo went to the Carrara marble quarries and
lived there for many months, getting out the
big blocks which were to be used in these
statues, but when he returned to Rome and
began his work the Pope vacillated ; some
one persuaded him that it was of ill omen for
a man to build his own tomb, and finally the
artist was torn from the task and set to fres-
coing the vault of the Sistine Chapel. It was
a bitter disappointment to him. Painting, he
insisted, was not his trade. It is hinted that
some of his rivals, fearing his success with the
sculpture of the tomb, instigated the Pope's
action, with the hope that his painting would
prove a failure. If that was their plot they
reckoned without their host. The Pope lived
to see the ceiling painted, but the tomb was
never finished. In his will he provided for

the completion of the work, and Michelangelo
was held to it by a contract that tormented
and tantalized him, and became the tragedy
of his life. They would never let him go on
with it; again and again succeeding popes
called him away for other tasks. The plan
was modified once or twice, and after thirty-
six years of heart-breaking suspense and dis-
traction the work was abandoned and Angelo
was released from his contract. The only
parts of the tomb that were completed were
the colossal Moses, so familiar to us all, and
two figures of captives, now in the Louvre.
Other figures were made from his designs,
but not by his hands.

Pope Leo X., the successor of Julius, was
a son of Lorenzo the Magnificent, and he
greatly desired to build architectural monu-
ments for his family and Florence, and commissioned Angelo to do the work. This, also,
was for the most part a disappointment and
weariness to him. His employers did not
know what they wanted, and the church of
San Lorenzo, whose façade he was to have
constructed, never was completed; after long
drudgery in the quarries preparing the marble for it, and laborious and vexatious delays,

Angelo was forced to abandon the labor, and the church " still stands," in the words of Mr. Sturgis, " with its brick wall as bare as if months of the precious life of a great artist had not been wasted in thought for it." [1] The great product of these years at Florence is gathered up in the tombs of the Medici, in the sacristy of this church, two groups in which the genius of the artist appears at its brightest.

The life of Angelo from his fortieth to his sixtieth year was full of confusion; he was traveling back and forth from Rome to Florence; much of the time he was kept at work for which he had no appetite; he was buffeted about by the orders of men who did not know their own minds. There was a revolution in Florence, in 1527, in which he took part; they made him engineer in chief, and he built the fortifications by which the city was defended. In 1534 Pope Paul III. called him back to Rome and set him to painting the vast fresco of the Last Judgment at the northern end of the Sistine Chapel. Finally, in 1546, he was made architect in chief of St. Peter's church, on which he labored until his

[1] Johnson's *Universal Cyclopedia*, v. 735.

death. The church had then been in course
of construction about forty years. Since his
day the building has been greatly altered, the
one grand feature which it owes to him is
the mighty dome, which is one of the architectural glories of the world.

In speaking now of a few of his greatest
works — for it is but few among them that I
can even name — my words must be for the
greater part a reflection of the judgment of
critics who have a right, which is not mine, to
estimate the art work of such a master. To
the least instructed of observers it is evident
that we have in all this work something that
does not appear in the classic marbles. The
sensuous beauty of the elder art gives place
to an intensity of life of which those ancient
sculptors had little conception. One thinks
of Paul's description of the period of thought-
less innocence, from which the knowledge of
the moral law roused him, and set in motion
the conflict between the lower and the higher
nature; the art of Greece shows us human
nature in that untroubled freedom, when men
were " alive without the law; " the art of
Angelo brings before us the poignant strivings
of a later day when "the commandment came,"

and the soul attained unto peace only through the mastery of the evil. If Dante, as Lowell tells us, was the first great Christian poet, Michelangelo is perhaps the first great artist whose work represents to us the struggle for redemption of the higher nature with the lower. It is the sense of this that finds expression in the critical moments on which his art is so apt to seize. Life, as he feels it, is a sublime conflict; it is not with blind fates that we are hopelessly contending ; the will is free and there is promise of victory, but it is a good fight, and there must be no flinching. There has been no mightier preacher of the strenuous life than Michelangelo.

Look at his David — the colossal statue of a youth ; the physical immaturity of adolescence is boldly represented. The moment is that in which the youth confronts the Philistine; his left hand upon the shoulder grasps the stone in the sling ; his right hand reaches back for the cord by which it is suspended ; he stands poised and ready for a tremendous effort; his face is full of the energy of resolve. It is not this instant, it is the next one, that the artist makes you see most clearly.

The block from which this statue was hewn had been under the chisel of another artist who had been attempting some colossal figure and had failed. It was placed, half hewn, in the hands of Angelo, and he saw the David in it. It is said that his work was somewhat cramped by the cutting of the other artist, but it is difficult to discover such defects in the statue.

The Medicean tombs are later and more remarkable productions. Each is an architectural construction, with pilasters and niches, placed against the marble wall of the sacristy; the figure of each Duke is seated in a niche above; and at the base of each are two reclining figures, couched on vacant sarcophagi; the one pair known as Day and Night, the other as Dawn and Twilight. The Medicean heroes overhead are masterpieces of plastic art, but they are rather subordinate characters, the strength of the work is in the symbolical figures. To some one who remarked upon this, Angelo is said to have replied, dryly, that probably no one would care very much about those Dukes after a few hundred years. He was quite right; there has been much dispute as to which is

Lorenzo of Urbino, and which Giuliano of
Nemours; neither of them was particularly
worth remembering.   The recumbent figures
at the base are, however, among the noblest
products of Angelo's art.   It was a dark
time for Florence when he conceived them —
a time when men were saying in the morning, " Would God it were even ! " and in the
evening, " Would God it were morning ! "
and Angelo has poured into these symbolic
figures all the passionate sadness of his soul.

" Standing before these statues," says Mr.
Symonds, " we do not cry, How beautiful !
We murmur, How terrible ! how grand !   Yet,
after long gazing, we find them gifted with
beauty beyond grace.   In each of them there
is a palpitating thought, torn from the artist's
soul and crystallized in marble.   It has been
said that architecture is petrified music.   In
the sacristy of San Lorenzo we feel impelled
to remember phrases of Beethoven.   Each
of these statues becomes for us a passion, fit
for musical expression, but turned, like Niobe,
to stone.   They have the intellectual vague-
ness, the emotional certainty, that belong to
the motives of a symphony.   In their alle-
gories, left without a key, sculpture has

passed beyond her old domain of placid, concrete form. The anguish of intolerable emotion, the quickening of the consciousness to a sense of suffering, the acceptance of the inevitable, the strife of the soul with destiny, the burden and the passion of mankind; — that is what they contain in their cold chisel-tortured marble. It is open to critics of the school of Lessing to object that here is the suicide of sculpture. It is easy to remark that those strained postures and writhen limbs may have perverted the taste of lesser crafts-men. Yet if Michelangelo was to carve Medicean statues after the sack of Rome and the fall of Florence, — if he was obliged in sober sadness to make sculpture a language for his sorrow-laden heart, — how could he have wrought more truthfully than this?" [1]

That such was the significance of these statues is made plain by the artist's own testimony. When the figure of the Night was first seen by the public a poet wrote this quatrain : —

" The Night thou seest here posed gracefully
   In act of slumber, was by an Angel wrought
   Out of this stone ; sleeping, with life she 's fraught ;
Wake her, incredulous wight : she 'll speak to thee."

[1] *Life of Michelangelo,* ii. 34.

Angelo himself, speaking for his statue, thus answered : —

" Grateful is sleep ; but still more sweet, while woe
   And shame endure, 't is to be stone like me,
   And highest fortune not to feel or see ;
Therefore awake me not : speak low ! speak low ! "

The legacy of art which Michelangelo has left to Rome is far too large for us to reckon. The Pieta, in St. Peter's, to which I have referred, — a statue of the Virgin holding in her lap the dead Christ, — is one of his most beautiful productions. The figure of the Moses is the best known of his statues; it represents him in the moment when he hears, on Mount Sinai, the noise of the idolatrous revelry in the valley below. " The majestic wrath of the figure," says Emerson, " daunts the beholder."

The two great works are the frescoes of the Sistine Chapel, — the crowd of historical and emblematic figures on the vaulting of the ceiling and the Last Judgment on the north wall above the altar. The frescoed ceiling is one of the most stupendous pieces of work ever undertaken by man. It is probable that the artist had assistance in the preparation of the plaster, and in the laying on of the color in some of the figures, but by far the larger part of the work was done by his own hands. The old story was that he finished it in twenty months, but that is not only incredible, it has been proven to be untrue. More than four years were consumed upon it, and that involves a feat sufficiently prodigious. Day after day, month after month, the painter lay upon his back upon the scaffold beneath the ceiling, looking upward and holding his brushes aloft; the strain upon his nerves was so great that his health was broken; for a long time it was nearly impossible for him to read without holding the book above the level of his eyes.

The Sistine Chapel is a long and narrow room, one hundred and thirty-two feet in length and forty-four in breadth; its ceiling is a flattened vault with no architectural divisions. The first work of the artist was therefore to paint upon this vault the representation of an architectural framework, with pilasters and brackets and ribbed arches, thus dividing the vast space so that his groups and figures might be distributed without confusion. The whole of this surface he covered with scenes from Bible history, with ideal

representations of Biblical and mythological
characters, and with a great number of lesser
figures, in all manner of attitudes.   Three
hundred and forty-three different representations of the human form, draped and undraped,
appear upon this ceiling, most of them life-size
and many of them colossal.   " To speak adequately of these form poems," says Symonds,
" would be quite impossible.   Buonarotti seems
to have intended to prove by them that the
human body has a language inexhaustible in
symbolism, every limb, every feature, and every
attitude being a word full of significance to
those who comprehend, just as music is a language whereof each chord and phrase has
correspondence with the spiritual world. . . .
This is how he closes one of his finest sonnets
to Vittoria Colonna : —

> ' Nor hath God deigned to show himself elsewhere
> More clearly than in human forms sublime,
> Which, since they image him, compel my love.'

. . . It may be asked what poems of action as
well as of feeling are to be expressed in this
form language ? The answer is simple. Paint
or carve the body of a man, and as you do it
nobly you will give the measure of both highest thought and most impassioned deed. This

is the key to Michelangelo's art. He cared
but little for inanimate nature. The landscapes of Italy, so eloquent in their beauty
and sublimity, were apparently a blank to
him. His world was the world of ideas, taking visible form, incarnating themselves in
man. One language the master had to serve
him in all need, the language of plastic human
form; but it was to him a tongue as rich in
its variety of accent and intonation as Beethoven's harmonies."

Taine, in a vivid description of the twenty
youthful figures seated upon the cornices of
the central frescoes, takes up the same theme :
" Who would suppose that the various attitudes of the human figure could affect the
mind with such diverse emotions ? The hips
actively support; the breast respires ; the entire covering of flesh strains and quivers;
the trunk is thrown back over the thighs, and
the shoulder ridged with muscles is about to
raise the impetuous arm. One of them falls
backward and draws his grand drapery over
his thigh, whilst another, with his arm over his
brow, seems to be parrying a blow. Others
sit pensive and meditating, with all their
limbs relaxed. Several are running and spring-

ing across the cornice or throwing themselves
back and shouting. You feel that they are
going to move and to act, yet you hope that
they will not, but maintain the same splendid
attitudes. Nature has produced nothing like
them, but she ought thus to have fashioned
the human race. In the ceiling of the Sistine
she might find all types; giants and heroes,
modest virgins, stalwart youths, and sporting
children; that charming ' Eve,' so young and
proud; that beautiful ' Delphic Sibyl ' who,
like some nymph of the Golden Age looks out
with eyes filled with innocent astonishment,
— all the sons and daughters of a colossal
militant race who preserved the smile, the se-
renity, the pure joyousness, the grace of the
Oceanides of Æschylus or the Nausicaa of
Homer. The soul of a great artist contains
an entire world within itself. Michelangelo's
soul is unfolded here on the Sistine ceiling." [1]

Of the other great painting, the " Last
Judgment," over the altar of the Sistine
Chapel, but the briefest mention can be made.
For eight years, between 1534 and 1542,
Angelo wrought upon it, pouring into it all
the bitterness and scorn of a deeply suffer-

[1] *Voyage en Italie.*

ing soul. The years just past had been
full of disaster to Italy; the land had been
overrun, Rome had been sacked by the Con-
stable of Bourbon; the scourge had fallen
upon the church, but no works meet for re-
pentance had appeared; the standards of conduct in the political and ecclesiastical world
were steadily sinking. In Germany and Switzerland and England the struggle of the Reformation was now in progress; the causes
which produced it were not less actively at
work in Italy. Michelangelo could not but
recall the terrible prophecies of Savonarola,
and their fiery threats of retribution are em-
bodied in the horrors of this gigantic picture.
In the midst of the scene the Christ as Judge
has risen from the cloud on which he has
been seated, his face is turned toward those
on his left hand, his right hand is lifted above
his head as if to hurl a thunderbolt; away
from him, staggering backward, plunging
downward, knotted together in the writhings
of despair, the lost souls are driven to their
doom; on the other side, wakened by the
trumpets of the seraphs, the dead are rising
from their graves and mounting upward to
confront the Judge; by the side of her Son

sits Mary with face averted, as if in pity.   It
is a dreadful picture; the *terribilità* of Michelangelo comes to its climax in it : there seems
to be no note of tenderness in all its stormy
harmonies ; and yet we know that it is the
great humanity of the master that inspired it
all — his holy indignation against the violence
and deceit and oppression whereof the earth,
as he saw it, was full.

In trying now to express some judgment of
the character of Michelangelo, we find a task
scarcely less difficult than that which confronts us when we estimate his art.   He is a
man of vast proportions and mighty energies ;
his temper is not less titanic than his designs ;
self - control is often wanting ; outbursts of
anger are frequent and fierce.   An ebullition
of this sort in his youth provoked a blow
which disfigured his face for life.   He is not
unjust, but he hates injustice and meanness
with a hatred which, if not perfect, is at least
adequate, and he scorches them with his wrath.
Sometimes, it must be owned, his resentments
are disproportionate to his provocations.
    In his early years in Rome his intimacies
were few.   For social pleasures he found lit-

tle time, and his habits were solitary. His tongue was keen, and some of his sharp sayings are memorable. When Pope Julius wanted him to adorn the figures of the ceiling with gold he answered, " Those apostles were poor men ; they wore no gold." Sebastian del Piombo was commissioned to paint a friar in a chapel. " He will spoil the chapel," said Angelo. " Why ? " they demanded. " When the friars have spoiled the world, which is so large," he said, " it is an easy thing for them to spoil such a tiny chapel." A painter produced a poor picture with one good figure — that of an ox. " Every artist draws his own portrait best," said Angelo.

Yet he was not always ill natured in his judgments of other artists. Some one asked him how he liked Donatello's statue of St. Mark at Florence. " I never saw a figure," he answered, " which so thoroughly represents a man of probity. If St. Mark was like that, we have reason to believe everything which he has said." To the martial figure of St. George, in the same place, his one word of appreciation was all that any artist could have asked for. " March ! " he cried.

Under his testy temper there was humor.

And there was tenderness. His fidelity to his kindred was exemplary. He was never married. " I have only too much of a wife in this art of mine," he testified. " She has always kept me struggling on. My children will be the works I leave behind me." His impecunious father and several scapegrace brothers were a heavy burden to him ; to his father he was always faithful and filial ; with his brothers he sometimes lost patience, but his long-suffering love failed not.

His own manner of life was most abstemious ; on himself he spent almost nothing ; to his relatives and dependents he was generous, almost to a fault.

With some of his brother artists his relations were kindly ; he loved and honored Titian ; he chid Cellini for trifling work, but praised him when he rose to the height of his calling. With Leonardo da Vinci, his townsman, he was not on good terms, and with Raphael, who was at work at Rome at the same time, he had but little to do ; jealousy or suspicion, on the one side or the other, kept them apart.

Perhaps the most sacred human influence that ever entered the life of Michelangelo

was a friendship of his later years with a
woman, Vittoria Colonna, the Marchioness of
Pescara. Her husband had perished years
before in battle; to his memory she was loyal,
and there was nothing of a purely sentimental
nature in her relations with Buonarotti. She
was a pure and high-souled woman, a poet
and a lover of art, with a religious nature
of great depth and tenderness. The days
of their friendship were the days when the
Reformation in northern Europe was shaking the old church to its centre, and with
this movement for the uprooting of ecclesiastical abuses, Vittoria Colonna and Michelangelo, although they never separated from
the church, were in deepest sympathy; much
of their converse was on these highest themes.
The friendship of this clear-minded, sound-
hearted woman was the greatest blessing that
ever came to Michelangelo; it was not until
his ripe maturity that he knew her; their
intimacy lasted barely eight years, and when
death separated them, Michelangelo, although
he had passed his threescore years and ten,
was to remain for sixteen years upon the
earth. Yet these last years, though shadowed by this sorrow, were surely better years

because hallowed by the memory of this noble woman.

Michelangelo had always been a poet; he knew how to use words for colors as well as colors for words, and in this affection for Vittoria the poetic instinct burst into bloom in his old age; the sonnets and madrigals that he addressed to her are full of spiritual beauty. This madrigal indicates the nature of their friendship : —

> " A man within a woman, nay, a god
> Speaks through her spoken word :
> I therefore, who have heard,
> Must suffer change, and shall be mine no more ;
> She lured me from the path I whilom trod.
> Borne from my former self by her away,
> I stand aloof, and mine own self deplore.
> Above all vain desire
> The beauty of her face doth lift my clay ;
> All lesser loveliness seems charnel mire.
> O lady, who through fire
> And water leadest souls to joys eterne,
> Let me no more unto myself return. " [1]

This, also, though not addressed, I like to believe was meant for her : —

> " Had I but earlier known that from the eyes
> Of the bright soul that fires me like the sun,
> I might have drawn new strength my race to run,
> Burning, as burns the phoenix ere it dies,

[1] Symonds's *Life*, ii. p. 121.

Even as the stag or lynx or leopard flies
To seek his pleasure or his pain to shun,
Each word, each smile of thine I would have won,
Flying, when now sad age all flight denies.

" Yet why complain ?   For even now I find
In that glad angel's face, so full of rest,
Health and content, heart's ease and peace of mind.
Perchance I might have been less simply blest,
Finding her sooner, if 't is age alone
That lets me soar with her to seek God's throne." [1]

It is a pathetic picture, the venerable Angelo bending by the couch of the dying Vittoria to kiss her cold hand, and then going away to the loneliness made sweet by her dear memory.

After her death his thoughts dwelt more and more on those themes of which they had communed ; the realities of the Christian faith became more vivid to him ; his fiery spirit was chastened by penitence and prayer, and he waited with eager expectation for the time of his release.   In these last days his Dante was always with him.   " Would to heaven," he said, " that I were such as he, even at the price of such a fate !   For his bitter exile and his virtue, I would exchange the most fortunate lot in the world."   " Toward the end,"

[1] *The Sonnets of Michael Angelo*, translated by Symonds, Portland ed. p. 55.

says Emerson, " there seems to have grown
in him an invincible appetite for dying." To
one who spoke to him sorrowfully of the end
that must come soon he answered : " No, it is
nothing ; for if life pleases us, death, being a
work of the same Master, ought not to dis-
please us." The resources of form and color
fail him as he stands so near to the confines
of the unseen and eternal, but he pours into
deathless verse the utterance of a faith that
could not fail : —

> " Now hath my life across a stormy sea,
> > Like a frail bark reached that wide port where all
> > Are bidden, ere the final reckoning fall
> > Of good and evil for eternity.
> Now know I well how that fond phantasy
> > Which made my soul the worshiper and thrall
> > Of earthly art is vain ; how criminal
> > Is that which all men seek unwillingly.
> Those amorous thoughts which were so lightly dressed,
> > What are they when the double death is nigh ?
> > The one I know for sure, the other dread.
> Painting nor sculpture now can lull to rest
> > My soul that turns to His great love on high,
> > Whose arms to clasp me on the cross were spread."

In such faith he died, February 18, 1564.
If he had lived sixteen days longer he would
have entered his ninetieth year. The Pope
decreed that his grave should be made at
Rome, but his kindred spirited the body away

by night and bore it to his beloved Florence, where they buried him with honor, and after months of costly preparation made him a splendid memorial pageant in the church where his greatest sculptures stand; all the artists of his native city brought offerings to enrich and beautify the catafalque erected to his memory, and orators and poets laid upon his tomb the garlands of their praise.

A great soul and glorious was Michelangelo Buonarotti, sculptor, painter, architect, poet; not exempt from frailties; possessing and deploring the defects of his qualities; but a heroic lover of Beauty; a loyal friend of Freedom and Justice; a clear witness for Truth; a humble servant of the Eternal One whose nature is light, whose law is liberty, whose name is love.

III

FICHTE, THE PHILOSOPHER

The true self, thinks Fichte, is something infinite. It needs a whole endless world of life to express itself in. Its moral law could n't be expressed in full on any one planet. Johann Gottlieb may be one of its prophets; but the heavens could not contain its glory and its eternal business. No one of us ever finally gets at the true Reason which is the whole of him. Each one of us is a partial embodiment, an instrument of the moral law, and our very consciousness tells us that this law is the expression of an infinite world life. The true self is the will which is everywhere present in things. This will is, indeed, the vine, whereof our wills are the branches. — *Josiah Royce.*

According to Fichte there is a " Divine Idea " pervading the visible Universe, which visible Universe is indeed but its symbol and sensible manifestation, having in itself no means, or even true existence independent of it. To the mass of men this Divine Idea of the world lies hidden; yet to discern it, to seize it, and to live wholly in it, is the condition of all genuine virtue, knowledge, freedom; and the end, therefore, of all spiritual effort in every age. — *Thomas Carlyle.*

JOHANN GOTTLIEB FICHTE

III

FICHTE, THE PHILOSOPHER

It is a long stride across the centuries from
the death of Michelangelo in 1564, to the
birth of Fichte in 1762. Many great things
have happened during this period; the Renaissance in Italy has spent its force; its prophet was buried in the grave of the great
Florentine sculptor, and a dismal decadence
has followed both in art and in letters, while
the national life of Italy has been practically
extinguished in the Spanish-Austrian domination. In the mean time, Germany, invigorated
by the Reformation, has been rising in intelligence and power; England, having lived
through the dynasty of the Tudors, and harvested the glories of the Elizabethan age, and
bidden welcome and good riddance to the
Stuarts, and rejoiced under the reign of William and Mary and good Queen Anne, is now
sitting down to endure the inglorious rule of
the third of the Georges, while thirteen Eng-

lish colonies, on this side of the sea, are beginning to feel themselves to be a people, and to lay the foundations of their national life.

Dante the poet, and Michelangelo the artist, have answered to our call as witnesses of the light; to-day we summon Fichte the philosopher. What is this philosophy of which he stands as a representative? The word is used variously; the restricted signification which we here assign to it is fairly conveyed by the title of one of Fichte's principal books, "Wissenschaftslehre,"— the science of knowledge. Philosophy, as the term is now generally used, is the endeavor to find out what we know and how we know it; to investigate the powers and processes of the human mind; to understand the significance of life. In another view it is an attempt to organize into general statements our knowledge of ourselves, and of the world in which we live, to unify the facts of our experience. We are all philosophers; we are all trying to find out the reason of things, the deeper meanings of life. The old farmer to whom Emerson had lent a volume of Plato was not making a very extravagant claim for himself when he said, on returning the book, " That old chap 's got some

o' *my* idees." His ideas they were, no doubt;
he had come by them honestly enough.

Nobody has said this any better than Professor Royce: " You philosophize when you
reflect critically on what you are actually doing in your world. What you are doing is,
of course, in the first place, living. And life
involves passions, faiths, doubts, and courage.
The critical inquiry into what all these mean
and imply is philosophy. We have our faith
in life ; we want, reflectively, to estimate this
faith. We feel ourselves in a world of law
and of significance. Yet why we feel this
homelike sense of the reality and worth of our
world is a matter for criticism. Such a criticism of life, made elaborate and thorough
going, is a philosophy."[1]

Much cheap satire is expended by crude
minds upon this attempt to explore the deep
things of life, but a great deal depends on our
solution of the fundamental problems of existence. It is true that men with absurd theories
of life have lived honorably, and that multi-
tudes whose theories are well enough are living basely ; whereupon some illogical minds
rush to the conclusion that there is no connec-

[1] *The Spirit of Philosophy,* pp. 1, 2.

tion between doctrine and practice, and that
what you think matters not. The truth simply
is that there is no *necessary* connection between doctrine and practice ; a man's practice
may disagree with his doctrine, but it generally agrees; and right thinking is more likely
than wrong thinking to result in right living.
To hold the contrary opinion is to repudiate
the first principles of rationality. The philosopher who helps us to know ourselves and the
significance of our own lives renders us, therefore, the highest possible service.   I trust that
we shall be able to see, as we study the life
of this German philosopher, how much brave
and clear thinking has to do in shaping the
lives of men and of nations.

Johann Gottlieb Fichte was born in Upper
Lusatia, a German province on the confines of
Saxony, Brandenburg, and Bohemia, in the
little village of Rammenau, May 19, 1762.
This province contains a large Slavic element,
but the Fichtes were originally Swedes; the
first of the name in those parts was a soldier
in the army of Gustavus Adolphus, who, in
one of the German campaigns of the great
Swedish king, was wounded and left behind
in Rammenau : the zealous Protestant family

that nursed him back to life gave him a home
and their daughter in marriage. It was a
sturdy and industrious line; Christian Fichte,
the philosopher's father, was a weaver of rib-
bons and a man of substance and character.
His first-born son was to him a wonder of
wonders; are not all children such to those
who have eyes to see? and the father gave
much of his leisure to the child, teaching him
to read, making him familiar with the Bible
and the Catechism, and telling him long tales
of his own *wander-jahre,* when, after the custom of the country he had been compelled to
be a journeyman indeed, traveling from town
to town in search of employment. Thus it
was that the child's mind was led out into the
wide world, and set upon its quest of knowledge. He seems to have been a very serious
boy, not much given to the sports of childhood; he was happiest alone in the fields and
the forests, thinking his own thoughts.

An incident of his childhood illustrates
the sensitive conscientiousness which, in after
years, caused him often to be misunderstood.
His father, as a reward of his industry, had
bought him the Story of Siegfried, and it enchanted him; his studies were forgotten. For

this he was sharply reproved, and in grief on account of his fault, he determined to destroy the book that it might no longer lead him into temptation. There was a bitter struggle in the child's heart as he stood by the brook, into which he was going to fling away his treasure, but conscience triumphed, and he flung it in, and then burst out crying. His father found him there weeping, and without waiting to find out why he had done it, punished him for throwing away the book. It was not the last time that he suffered bitterly and unjustly for simple fidelity to his highest convictions.

The kindly Protestant pastor of the village soon got his eye on this exceptional child and gave him such help as he could. Finding him keenly attentive to the Sunday services, he asked him one day to tell him what he could remember of what he had heard the preceding Sunday. The child promptly gave him a good part of the discourse with the Scripture texts by which the argument had been confirmed. A miracle like that in a rustic community soon becomes village gossip; a nobleman from abroad, visiting the lord of the manor, providentially expresses his regret on Sunday afternoon that he had not heard the morning sermon. "Easy enough to supply that want," they tell him. "There is a little boy in a cottage near by who heard it, and who can, no doubt, repeat it to you." "Send for him," says the baron; and young Johann Gottlieb, aged seven, in a linen pinafore, with a big nosegay in his hand for the lady of the house, comes in and recites, fluently and clearly, the morning discourse. "This child," says the baron, "is a marvel; let him go home with me and he shall be set forward in the ways of learning." With many misgivings the parents resign their boy to the keeping of the good Freiherr von Militz, who bears him away to his seat at Liebeneichen, not far from Miessen. It was a great and stately house in the midst of a gloomy forest country: the boy was away from his mother; no wonder he nearly died from homesickness. But the kind-hearted Freiherr found him a home in the family of a Protestant pastor in the little village of Niederau, near by, and the boy was happy again. It was a good home for him; the minister had no children of his own, and he loved children, and little Johann Gottlieb was a child to love. The Herr Pastor was his preceptor ; through the elementary studies and the beginnings of Greek and Latin the lad went swiftly ; soon the pupil was beyond his master's help, and in his twelfth year they sent him to the Schulpforta, near Raumberg.

It was one of those mediæval schools in which the paths of learning are made as thorny as possible ; teachers and pupils dwelt in cells ; once a week only the prisoners were let out to visit, under the eye of a detective, a playground in the vicinity. It is not related that they were permitted to play ; perhaps this was simply a method of torture. The fagging system was here in vogue, and the senior to whom Fichte was committed was a young brute to whom tyranny was a recreation. It was a stern discipline for the lonely youth ; there was nothing in the intellectual or the moral atmosphere of the school which was not depressing : " his sadness and tears," says a biographer, " exposed him to the derision of his school-fellows, and he, shy and retiring, shrunk within himself, restrained his tears, or suffered them to flow only in secret. Here, however, he learned the useful lesson of self-reliance, so well, though so bitterly, taught by the absence of sympathy in those around us ; and from this time to the end of his life it was never forgotten."

By some means a copy of " Robinson Crusoe" found its way into the hands of this lonely lad, and he promptly resolved that he, too, would fly to some desert island — anywhere, anywhere, out of that world. He will not sneak away ; he tells his senior that if the tyranny is not abated he is going, and gets scoffed at, of course ; then he takes up his journey. The world is before him and the place of torment is behind him ; but he remembers the counsel of the good Herr Pastor never to do any serious thing without prayer, and he falls on his knees by the roadside. Now he thinks of his parents ; their well-imagined grief unnerves him ; he turns back to meet his pursuers, and is taken before the Rector of the school, to whom he tells the whole story so ingenuously that he is not only not punished but is taken by that functionary under his special protection. From this time forward the lines fall to him in less desolate places ; a new spirit seemed to have taken possession of the school ; petty tyrannies and small dishonesties gave place to a manlier and more magnanimous temper. The school bears now, we are told, little of its ancient character; who shall say how much the high-mindedness of this boy had to do with its reformation?

In his eighteenth year he entered the University of Jena; here and in Leipsic he completed his university course. But theology as then taught gave him little more than a fit of intellectual indigestion; he must go deeper than these doctors dared to venture. The first *cul de sac* into which they led him was the old dilemma of predestination and free will; with logic for his vehicle he came out, of course, a stout determinist.

Shortly after he left the University and while he was still struggling in the philosophical bog, his kind benefactor died, and he was left penniless to make his own way in the world. Tutoring in families was the only avocation that opened to him : the living thus gained was precarious; often he was on the verge of starvation. Four years of this fighting with adverse fate gave him chances enough to cultivate a practical philosophy, chances that he did not miss. Young men of brains and training sometimes find it hard in these

days to get employment; few of them have
passed through a struggle for life more severe
than that in which Fichte was engaged during
the four years after he left the University,
and none of them more manfully. In the
spring of 1788 his resources were at the lowest ebb; for such service as he could render
there seemed to be no demand. "It is the
eve," says a biographer, "of his birthday in
this same month of May. The pensive fancy
figures him walking disconsolately about the
environs of Leipsic, the balmy evening air
blowing fresh upon his cheek; birds of various
note warbling softly their May night vespers
or nestling, with placid murmurings, in the
fields. He walks, as we said, disconsolately;
pondering with unavailing anxiety all the pro-
jects which it has entered into his mind to
devise, and finds them all alike hopeless. The
world has cast him out, his country has refused him bread; this approaching birthday,
for aught he can tell, may be his last. Doubtless people have died of starvation; why not
he? Full of bitter thoughts he returns, as
it appears likely, for the last time, to his solitary and uncheerful dwelling. Can this be
really a letter lying on the table? Yes, Fichte,

even so : or say rather a hastily written note,
a note from friend Weisse, the tax collector,
requesting thee to step over to his house without delay. What can so peremptory a summons signify ? It turns out that friend Weisse
is authorized to make him the offer of a tutorship in a private family in Zurich."

The place will not be open before September, but by some means, perhaps by the same
friend's assistance, he is enabled to subsist until
August, and then, too poor to pay coach fare,
but with a little money in his pocket to buy
bread and shelter, he sets out on foot for
Switzerland, a good three hundred miles as
the crow flies, farther, doubtless, by such roads
as he must travel. We do not know the route :
possibly it took him through the picturesque
Franconia hills, and old Bayreuth, and the
more ancient Nürnberg ; we are only sure that,
though often footsore and weary, he was heart-
whole and happy, for honorable work and
livelihood were awaiting him at his journey's
end.

The two years of his residence in Zurich
were memorable years ; his work kept him too
busy for much general study, but he preached
now and then, with great acceptance, we are

told, and the friendships that he formed were
of lasting influence upon his life. Into the
family of a certain local notability named
Rahn he had the entrée; Rahn's wife, who
was now dead, had been the sister of the poet
Klopstock, who had once lived here in Zurich
and who, by the way, had been a pupil of that
Purgatorio at Pforta where Fichte prepared
for the University. In this family the distinguished Lavater was a constant visitor; this
intense but erratic genius must have greatly
stimulated the mind of this budding philosopher. The two years in Zurich were momentous to Fichte for many reasons, chief of which
was his betrothal to Johanna Rahn, daughter
of the house in which he had spent so many
agreeable hours, and niece of the poet Klopstock. It was a romantic and beautiful attachment; the love-letters, which began while
he was still in Zurich, and which continued
through the years of separation, are utterances
of ardent affection and high philosophy and
strenuous purpose. In the spring of 1790 his
engagement as tutor is at an end and he turns
his face homeward, traveling again most of
the way on foot, but bearing with him some
strong testimonials by means of which he

hopes to find employment. He goes to Stutt-
gart and finds nothing; to Weimar with equal
success: Herder is sick and Goethe is in Italy
and Schiller is too busy to see callers. So
back he goes to Leipsic and waits. There is
a little teaching to do, and there is a project
of a monthly magazine, with high aims, which
never materializes, and there is strenuous endeavor, which is wholly futile, to get a little
money by his pen. How he manages to keep
soul and body together we are not clear; but
something happens to him in the course of the
winter which is even more important than
keeping body and soul together; it is the dis-
covery of the truth which establishes at once
and forever his intellectual integrity; which
shows him the significance of life, and makes
his vocation clear as the daylight. That dis-
covery comes to him through reading the
" critical philosophy " of Immanuel Kant.
His beliefs, until now, had been in confusion;
his theories had been at war with his convictions. So writes he to his Johanna, in the
winter of 1790 : —

" A circumstance which seemed dependent
on mere chance led me to give myself up to
the study of the Kantian philosophy, — a phi-

losophy that restrains the imagination (which, in my case, was always too powerful), gives reason the dominion, and raises the soul to an elevation above earthly concerns. I have accepted a new and nobler morality; and, instead of occupying myself with outward things, I am employed more exclusively with my own being. This has given me a peace such as I have never before experienced, for amid uncertain worldly prospects I have spent my happiest days. I propose to devote some years of my life to this philosophy, and all that I write, at least for some time to come, shall have reference to it. It is difficult, beyond conception, and stands greatly in need of simplification. The principles, indeed, are hard speculations, having no direct bearing on human life, but their consequences are extremely important to an age whose morality is corrupted at the very fountain; and to set these consequences before the world in a clear light would, I believe, be doing it good service. . . . I am now thoroughly convinced that the human will is free, and that to be happy is not the purpose of our being, but to deserve happiness." [1]

[1] *Popular Works of Fichte*, edited by Wm. Smith, i. 40.

So Fichte has found his vocation. It will be months and years before he will be able to apply himself to it, but he knows what is his high calling ; his mind has found the centre of light, and his heart is at rest in the assurance of a pure love; what more can any man covet? All else is but accident or appendage.

Need enough is there of this calm philosophy, for the hosts of adverse circumstance are not yet put to rout. There is great hope in the spring of 1791 that he may be able to claim his Johanna and set up his home, but that is dashed to the ground ; then, in far-off Warsaw work is offered and he trudges thither to find that the situation is impossible. But Königsberg is not far away ; before he turns homeward he must go thither and see the great philosopher who has led him into the light.

Conceive the ardent neophyte seeking out the little, fussy old bachelor philosopher in his out-of-the-way home in Königsberg. Doubtless, in the outward shape and life of the great man there may have been disillusion for Fichte. " I do not believe," says Heine, " that the great cathedral clock [of Königsberg] accomplished its day's work in a less passionate or more regular way than its countryman, Immanuel Kant. Rising from bed, coffee-drinking, eating, walking, everything had its fixed time ; and the neighbors knew that it must be exactly half past four when they saw Professor Kant in his gray coat, with cane in his hand, move toward the little lime-tree avenue which is named after him ' The Philosopher's Walk.' Eight times he walked up and down that walk at every season of the year, and when the weather was bad or the gray clouds threatened rain, his servant, old Lampe, was seen anxiously following him with a large umbrella under his arm, like an image of Providence."

One can easily guess that the reception given to the young Fichte by this preoccupied philosopher was not over-cordial ; doubtless Kant had too many interruptions. But Fichte greatly wishes to secure between himself and his great master what he calls a " free scientific confidence," so he sits down in Königsberg and writes his first considerable treatise, " The Critique of all Revelation." With this key he will unlock the heart of Kant. " It is perhaps one of the most touching and instructive passages of literary history," says William Smith, " to find a young man at a distance from his own country, without a friend, without even the means of personal subsistence, and sustained only by an ardent and indomitable love of truth, devoting himself with intense application to the production of a systematic work on one of the deepest subjects of philosophic thought, that he might thereby attain the friendship and confidence of one whom he regarded as the greatest of living men." [1] The philosopher looks it over and cautiously commends it, but the performance does not greatly forward the desired " free scientific confidence." Meanwhile Fichte's slender resources are completely exhausted, and he is far from home. But the sun never sets on a resolute spirit; now when his need is deepest, an invitation comes from Dantzic, still farther north, upon the shores of the Baltic, and he hastens ·to find a congenial home as private tutor in the family of Count von Krokow. Now a publisher is found for " The Critique of all Revelation," and the book, published, by an accident, anonymously, is seized upon by the critics as undoubtedly a publication of the redoubtable Kant himself. Kant quickly sets that right and proclaims the true author ; so

[1] Fichte's *Popular Works*, ii. 49, 60.

here at once is recognition and renown. The critics cannot take it back; they have said it; it is a book that Kant may, nay — must have written; this writer, then, is worthy to rank with the greatest philosopher of modern history. The door which has hitherto been shut and bolted in Fichte's face is now at least ajar; the steady pressure of dauntless industry will force it open.

In the summer of 1793, and in the thirty-second year of his life, he is able to return to Zurich and take into his home the woman who has waited for him so loyally. With the small dowry she brings him and his own modest earnings he is free of the world; he can go on with his study unhindered.

He tarries here in Zurich for a year, studying and writing; now comes an invitation from royalty to undertake the education of the Prince of Mecklenburg-Strelitz, a court position with distinction a plenty, and pudding galore, but he will none of it. "I desire nothing," he says, "but leisure to execute my plan; then fortune may do with me what it will." Next arrives an invitation from Jena to become a supernumerary Professor of Philosophy there, and that is another story. At once he accepts it, and is soon at work in the most illustrious of all the seats of learning in Germany. Weimar, the capital and court of the Grand Duke Charles Augustus, is only a dozen miles away, and the University is the Grand Duke's pride; he has gathered about him such a galaxy of genius as has not more than once or twice been grouped upon the planet — by Pericles, perhaps, at Athens, and by Lorenzo the Magnificent at Florence. At this court and in this University, now, between the years 1790 and 1810, at the zenith of its fame, men like Wieland, Reinhold, Goethe, Schiller, Schlegel, Oken, Hegel are gathered; into this august company Johann Gottlieb Fichte enters May 18, 1794. So great are the expectations concerning him that the largest hall in Jena is crowded to the roof on his first appearance as a lecturer, and numbers are turned away. The impression which he made, says one reporter, exceeded all expectation. " His singular and commanding address, his fervid and impetuous eloquence, the profoundness and rich profusion of his thoughts, poured forth in the most convincing sequence and fashioned with a wondrous precision, astonished and delighted his hearers. His

triumph was complete; he left the hall the
most popular professor of the greatest University in Germany."

But university popularity, as other professors have found, is a fitful gust; no man
can tell which way it will blow to-morrow. In
no other German University was the lawless-
ness — sometimes called *Freiheit* — of student
life more flagrant than in Jena; mobs of
Burschen frequently broke into houses of
professors and other residents and robbed the
wine-cellars to furnish forth their own ca-
rousals; neither the dignity of man nor the
helplessness of woman was any protection
against their brutalities. To the lofty manliness of Fichte such a state of things was intolerable, and he determined to appeal to the
students themselves to put away these barbarities. His lectures on Academical Morality, simply by lifting up a higher ideal, produced a marked effect; the students responded
to the appeal and offered to abolish their
unions and abandon their atrocities, but the
authorities of the University, apparently jealous of the fame of Fichte, fumbled with the
business, and the result was that one of the
three students' unions refused to lay down its

weapons of war, and remained as a disturbing element. But Fichte determined to continue his lectures, and he desired to give them at an hour not occupied by other instruction, that all the students might attend. Would Sunday morning do? That question greatly agitated the University authorities. Finally, Professor Schütz, who seems to have been a Daniel come to judgment, ventured the query: "If plays are permitted on Sunday, why not moral lectures?" and that seems to have settled it.

But there are worse foes to fight than rowdy students; intolerant conservatism brings first the charge that he is attempting to undermine Christianity and substitute therefor the worship of reason, and when that charge is exploded, returns to the attack with the accusation of atheism. The absurdity of it! It is probably safe to say that there is no man in Germany whose faith in God is so strong as that of Johann Gottlieb Fichte. You might almost say that he believes in nothing else; it might plausibly be made a charge against his philosophy that it leaves no adequate room in the universe for other personalities. On this Fichte will neither explain nor apologize; he tells the University authorities

that they must either acquit him absolutely or
accept his resignation, and his peremptory
tone, rather than any belief in the justice of
the accusation, provokes them to take him at
his word and let him go.

Once more he is adrift, but the port is near.
King Frederick William III., grand-nephew
of Frederick the Great, and great grand-uncle
of the present Kaiser, is told of Fichte's mis-
hap at Jena, and bids him welcome to Berlin ;
he is not afraid of the heresy : " *Mir thut
das nichts !* " he laughs. So Fichte once
more strikes his tent and, in July, 1799,
pitches it in the Prussian capital, thencefor-
ward to be his home save for some temporary
residence at the University of Erlangen in
Bavaria. Poverty was still his constant companion ; some small revenue may have come
from the books he printed, and from courses
of private lectures, but the housekeeping must
have been of a very simple sort; the living
was the plainest but the thinking was the
highest. Here he completed and published,
in 1799, his book on " The Vocation of Man,"
— in the spirit that animates it one of the
noblest books of all literature. Here, also, in
the years that immediately follow, are made

ready for the press the books by which he will
be longest remembered, his lectures on " The
Vocation of the Scholar," and " The Nature
of the Scholar," and his lectures on " The
Way to the Blessed Life, or the Doctrine of
Religion." Of these, the substance of the
first two was given to the students of Jena.
Here was gathered about him a circle of
brilliant companions, — Friedrich and Wil-
helm Schlegel, Tieck, Woltmann, Kotzebue,
Reichhardt, Bernhardt, Jean Paul Friedrich
Richter.

It may be well to pause here for a word
upon the contribution which Fichte has made
to the science of knowledge and upon the
nature of his teaching.

His system of thought is sometimes described as subjective idealism; it is better
named, as Professor Royce suggests, ethical
idealism, for the heart and soul of it is in the
recognition of human freedom. " Vocation "
is Fichte's great word — " The Vocation of
the Scholar," " The Vocation of Man," are
phrases in his view of supreme significance.
Man is not the creature of circumstance, his
precise business in the world is to control

and command circumstances, to impress his
will upon them. His will is, indeed, for him,
the fundamental reality; for it is only by
his effort to express himself that he becomes
aware of his own existence and of existences
other than himself. "The deepest truth, then,"
— this is Professor Royce's exposition, —
"is a practical truth. I need something
not myself, in order to be active, that is, to
exist. My very existence is practical; it is
self-assertion. I exist, so to speak, by hurling
the fact of my existence at another than myself. I limit myself thus, by a foreign, somewhat opaque external, my own opposite; but
my limitation is the free choice of my own
self. By thus limiting myself, I give myself
something to do, and thus win my own very
existence. Yet this opposition, upon which
my life is based, is an opposition within my
deepest nature. I have a foreign world as
the theatre of my activity; I exist only to
conquer and to win that apparently foreign
world to myself; I must come to possess it;
I must prove that it is mine. In the process
of thus asserting a foreign world, and then
actively identifying it as not foreign and external, but as our own, our life itself consists.

This is what is meant by work, by love, by duty." [1]

As a consistent idealist Fichte, of course, denies that the external world has any independent existence or validity; each of us makes his own world. There are no realities of knowledge except God and myself, and the self in me is but a manifestation of God. Outside of me there is a limit in resisting which I come to myself; but the impulse which sends me out toward this limit and thus brings me to self-consciousness is " God working in me, to will and to work of his good pleasure." " This universe of selves " — I am again leaning on Professor Royce — " constitutes the life and embodiment of the one true and infinite Reason, God's will, which, itself supreme and far above the level of our finite personality, uses even our conscious lives and wills as part of its own life. This doctrine Fichte himself, in one of his later works ('The Way to the Blessed Life '), identifies with the teaching of the Fourth Gospel. According to this view, you see, God, in so far as He reveals himself, is indeed the vine, and we, in so far as we truly

[1] *The Spirit of Modern Philosophy,* p. 158.

live, are the sap-laden and fruitful branches.
The only real world is the world of conscious
activity, and so of spiritual relationships, of
society, of serious business, of friendship, of
love, of law, of rational existence, — in a
word, of work; as for matter, that is the
mere show-stuff that is needed to embody, to
express, to give form, stability, outline, as it
were, to our moral work." [1]

Let me borrow from Professor Everett one
more word of interpretation : —

"The world is the projection of human
spirits and represents the stage which they
have reached. God is practically recognized
as an ideal; and may thus be seen in absolute
beauty and completeness. One can doubt His
reality and His perfection no more than he
can doubt his own being. At the same time
it is affirmed, from the beginning, that it is by
the Divine life within, that the spirit presses
on toward the Divine Ideal. In regard to this
impulse within us, there can be as little doubt
as in regard to the ideal toward which it points.
God is thus recognized as the most certain of
realities. The ideal to which the soul aspires
is infinite. So soon as one form has been

[1] *The Spirit of Modern Philosophy*, p. 153.

attained, another and higher takes its place. In the fact of its impulse to attain to this ideal, the spirit finds the pledge of its own immortality." [1]

It is impossible to present in this curt fashion any adequate account of the philosophy of Fichte. It is more to our purpose to grasp the great ideas which controlled his teaching and the great ends of which he never lost sight. However defective may have been his metaphysics, one commanding truth held possession of the man and reverberates through all his utterances. To say that he believed in God would be quite misrepresenting his mental attitude; God was to him the most certain fact of knowledge. Matthew Arnold's two great phrases, — " that stream of tendency by which all things strive to fufill the law of their being," and " the Power not ourselves that makes for righteousness," — would both have fitted his thoughts fairly well; though he would hardly, perhaps, have been willing to say that the Power is not ourselves; rather would he have held that it is one with our real selves, and finds its highest revelation through us.

[1] Fichte's *Science of Knowledge — A Critical Exposition*, p. 273.

The one central, supreme, all-comprehend-
ing fact of our individual lives, of the life of
the world, in Fichte's doctrine, is God. The
Divine Idea is striving after fulfillment in us
as individuals, in the societies which we form,
in the states of which we are citizens. Yet
we are free, and it is for us to work out our
own salvation by discerning the Divine Idea,
and conforming our own purposes to it. Ten-
nyson's prayer paraphrases his thought : —

> " Our wills are ours, we know not how ;
> Our wills are ours to make them thine."

The divine lineaments are impressed on every
human life ; the divine purpose is seeking expression in every human character : we must
find it in ourselves and lay hold upon it and
rejoice in it, and fight against everything in
ourselves or in the world about us that hinders
its development. We must find it in others,
and make them apprehend it, and stimulate
and strengthen it in every possible way.

This sublime truth of the immanent God is
something more than a mystical speculation
with Fichte : he seeks to bring it home to
every man's business and bosom, to make it
the ruling idea of every individual and of
every social organization. Those untamed

Burschen of Jena — he drives this truth into
their heads with irresistible logic. It is not
in the hortatory fashion ; he does not preach ;
he expounds and elucidates and enforces ; he
makes them see that it must be so. There
is passionate intensity behind it all ; there is
tremendous conviction ; it is a man that is
speaking and not a mere reasoning machine ;
but, after all, the method is scientific ; it is not
the speaker who claims their assent but the
truth spoken. There is one thing for them
to do, one only, for every one of them — to
discern the Divine Idea struggling for utterance in their own lives and live by it ; nothing
else is life. In all these great lectures on the
Nature and Vocation of the Scholar, and in
the book on " The Way to the Blessed Life,"
the same note is always resounding. Phillips
Brooks used to say that he had but one sermon, and Fichte might have said the same
thing : indeed, Fichte's sermon and Brooks's
were much the same sermon.

But the quiet life of the cloister and the
lecture room at Berlin and Erlangen are rudely
interrupted. Napoleon is marching over Europe ; most of the German states have fallen
before him ; Prussia, which has resisted to

the last, is now threatened by advancing
hosts. Fichte begs of the King permission
to go out with the army against the foe; he
cannot fight, but he conceives that as patriotic orator he might kindle the souls of his
countrymen. He laments, as he says, " that
his age has denied him the privilege accorded
to Æschylus and Cervantes, to make good
his words by manly deeds. . . . But since he
may only speak he would speak fire and sword.
Nor would he do this securely and away from
all danger." Philosophy is not, you see, with
Fichte, a mere abstraction. The Divine Idea,
as he incarnates it, includes the might of the
Lord of Sabaoth. The rapid progress of the
war forbade, however, the fulfillment of his
chivalric hope; the battle of Jena was fatal
to the Prussians; Napoleon entered Berlin,
and Fichte, disdaining to live in his own
home at the mercy of the invader, fled to
Königsberg and thence to Copenhagen, re-
maining until the humiliating peace of Tilsit
permitted him to return to a nation robbed of
much of its territory and trampled beneath
the heel of the conqueror.

But this was the hour of the rebirth of the
nation. The Teutonic spirit could not endure

this shame. These losses must be retrieved
and this dishonor must be wiped out. But
how and by whose hands? That was the
burning question. And the answer — the
answer that the people heard, that convinced
their understanding, that guided their purpose, that kindled in their souls a quenchless
resolution, was spoken most clearly by Johann
Gottlieb Fichte. Other hearts burned with
the same enthusiasm, other lips glowed with
a kindred message, but the testimony seems
to be clear that no voice was so influential as
his in the crisis of the nation. It was not an
economist, nor a jurist, nor a diplomatist, nor
a soldier, who pointed out to Prussia the only
way of life; it was this humble scholar and
teacher, this poor man of books and ideas,
who proved that he had understanding of the
times and could show his countrymen what
they ought to do. His Lectures to the German People — " Reden an Deutschen " — delivered at this juncture, are one of the great
events of German history — more significant,
more decisive of national destiny, perhaps,
than any battle ever won by German arms.
What was the burden of this prophecy? Simply the old truth that he has been telling so

diligently in his lectures on the Vocation of the Scholar and the Vocation of the Man — this people must know God's will and do it. It was their manhood that needed invigoration ; they must be better men ; they must have clearer minds and stronger wills, and a deeper sense of their vocation. Not to military skill and prowess, not even to an increased economic efficiency did he direct their thoughts, but to the things that are unseen and eternal; salvation must come to the nation through the recognition of spiritual aims, through the culture of moral dignity, and through fidelity to the great ideals of freedom and character.

In one passage of lofty eloquence he summons the spirits of their ancestors, who, in the primeval forests, " stemmed with their own bodies the tide of Roman domination over the world, who vindicated with their own blood the independence of those mountains, plains, and streams which you have suffered to fall a prey to the stranger. They call to you, ' Be ye our defenders ! hand down our memory to future ages, honorable and spotless as it has come down to you. Hitherto our struggle has been deemed noble, great, and wise ;

we have been looked upon as the consecrated
and inspired ones of a Divine World Plan.
Should our race perish with you, then will our
honor be changed into dishonor, our wisdom
into folly.   For if Germany were ever to be
subdued to the Empire, then were it better
to have fallen before the elder Romans than
their modern descendants.   We withstood
those and triumphed ; these have scattered you
like chaff before them.   But as matters now
are with you, seek not to conquer with bodily
weapons, but stand firm and erect before them
in spiritual dignity.   Yours is the greater destiny, — to found an empire of mind and reason ; to destroy the dominion of rude physical
power as the ruler of the world.   Do this, and
you shall be worthy of your descent from us.' "

Are you listening, Kaiser Wilhelm II., War
Lord of Germany ?

" All ages " — the orator goes on — " all
the wise and good who have ever breathed
the air of this world of ours — all their
thoughts and aspirations toward a higher good
mingle with these voices and encompass you
about and raise supplicating hands toward
you.   Providence itself, if we may venture so
to speak, and the Divine Plan in the creation

of the human race, which indeed only exists
that it may be understood of men and by men
be wrought out into reality, plead with you to
save their honor and existence." [1]

It was not a prudent thing for Fichte thus
to speak. Berlin was still occupied by French
troops, tarrying here until the heavy indem-
nity could be raised and paid; the trumpets
of their battalions marching by often drowned
his voice while he was speaking, and spies
mingled with his audiences, but he faltered
not. " The good that I seek," he said, " is
the awakening and elevation of the people,
against which my personal danger is not to be
reckoned, but for which it may rather be most
advantageously incurred. My family and my
son shall not want the support of the nation —
the least of the advantages of having a martyr
for their father. This is the best choice. I
could not devote my life to a better end." [2]

Not in vain were these lofty appeals to the
heart of the German nation. Nor was it a
mere emotional awakening. The first remedy for their miseries that suggested itself was
the education of the people. In these very

[1] Fichte's *Popular Works*, i. 152-156.
[2] Fichte's *Popular Works*, i. 150.

addresses Fichte first proposed and clearly outlined that system of popular education which is the chief element of German power and prosperity to-day. One of the first things determined on was the establishment of a new university based on more modern ideas, and Fichte was requested to draft a plan for it. His ideas were not all accepted ; they contemplated a kind of organic unity in the work of the university, and a degree of devotion to the culture of character as the main purpose of academic instruction for which his contemporaries were hardly ready ; but when the university was organized by the suffrages of his fellow professors, — such men as Wolff, Humboldt, De Wette, Schleiermacher, Neander, and Savigny, — he was unanimously elected the first rector. The greatest university of Europe owns him to-day as chief among its founders and its first official head. In this position he gave himself, with dauntless enthusiasm, to the ethical and spiritual culture of the student body, — to the creation among them of standards of honor and manliness before which the barbarities of student life should disappear.[1]

[1] William Smith, in his Memoir, makes Fichte the first rector ; R. Adamson, in his *Fichte*, gives that honor to

Under such inspiring influences Prussia is roused, quickened, regenerated; Stein is the statesman under whom the renovation is well begun. Great social reforms are set in motion, serfdom is abolished, schools are opened, a new heart and a new purpose have taken possession of the nation; and when, on Napoleon's retreat from Moscow, the hour strikes for the deliverance of the people, they rise as one man; there is an energy of patriotic resolve against which no force can stand.

It is in the beginning of this campaign that the students of the new university gather one day to hear Professor Fichte speak on Duty. Great is the throng, and more or less turbulent and flippant, but there is a hush when the Herr Professor stands up, for all are full of expectation. " He lectures," says an enthusiastic reporter who was there, " with his usual dignity and calmness, rising at intervals into fiery bursts of eloquence, but governed always by a wondrous tact of logic such as few could equal. From this topic of duty in the abstract he leads his audience to the pre-

Schmalz. It is possible that Fichte acted as rector of the earlier and later organization, and that Schmalz was placed at its head when it was more formally organized.

sent state of national affairs. On them he
glows and expands with animation, the rolling of drums without frequently drowning
his voice but inspiring him with fresh courage to proceed. He paints the desolation of
the country, the withering hideousness of
usurpation; he swells with a sublime indignation against oppressors, and passionately enforces it as the duty of every one before him
to consecrate his individual strength and faculty to the rescue of his native land. 'Gentlemen,' he exclaims finally, 'this course of
lectures will be suspended till the end of the
campaign. We will resume them in a free
country or die in the attempt to establish our
liberties.' The hall reverberates with loud
responsive shoutings; the rolling of the outward drums is answered by the clapping of
innumerable hands and the stampings of a
thousand feet; every German heart there
present is moved to resolution and pants for
conquest or for martyrdom. Fichte descends
from his place, passes through the crowd, and
places himself in the ranks of a corps of vol-
unteers then departing for the army."

The campaign, as you all know, ended with
the destruction of Napoleon and the rehabili-

tation of Prussia; it was the first resolute and mighty step onward in a national career which has made Prussia the arbiter of the destinies of Germany, which has united the German people, and placed upon the head of the successor of Fichte's king the crown of a mighty empire.

It was not for Fichte to render any important service in the army, but he had done better than that; more than almost any man in Germany he had helped to make the army possible, and to fill it with the faith that made it victorious. His devoted wife, nursing the sick soldiers in the hospital that winter, was smitten with a malignant fever; her husband nursed her through it, only leaving her side long enough to meet his class in the evening. One night he went to his work, hardly hoping to find her alive on his return; he came back to find the fever broken, and in his joy stooped to kiss her, thus drawing in the poisoned breath that prostrated him with the same deadly malady. For eleven days he lingered, most of the time under the shadow. In one of his lucid intervals they told him of Blücher's passage of the Rhine and of the final expulsion of the French army from German soil. One moment of exultation, then the delirium returned and he was fighting in the ranks and shouting with the victors. Rest came to him, at last, January 27, 1814, in the fifty-second year of his age, while his eye was not yet dim nor his natural force abated.

What was this man? Let him answer for himself: "To this am I called, — to bear witness to the Truth : my life, my fortunes are of little moment; the results of my life are of infinite moment. I am a Priest of Truth : I am in her pay; I have bound myself to do all things, to venture all things, to suffer all things for her. If I should be hated and persecuted for her sake, if I should even meet death in her service, what wonderful thing is it I shall have done, — what but that which I clearly ought to do."[1]

If we might speak for him we would say that he came to open men's eyes to the meaning of the life they are living, to help them to discern and rejoice in their inheritance as the sons of God. More comprehensive thinkers, more careful analysts of the soul there may have been among German philosophers, but no truer witness, no manlier man. "We state

[1] Fichte's *Popular Works*, i. 224.

Fichte's character," says Carlyle, "as it is known and admitted by men of all parties among the Germans, when we say that so robust an intellect, a soul so calm, so lofty, massive, and immovable has not mingled in philosophical discussion since the time of Luther. . . . The man rises before us, amid contradiction and debate, like a granite mountain amid clouds and wind. . . . Fichte's opinions may be true or false, but his character, as a thinker, can be slightly valued only by such as know it all; and as a man, approved by action and suffering, in his life and in his death, he ranks with a class of men who were common only in better ages than ours." [1]

In a churchyard, just inside the Oranienburg-Thor, in Berlin, is an obelisk reared to his memory with this inscription : —

THE TEACHERS SHALL SHINE
AS THE BRIGHTNESS OF THE FIRMAMENT ;
AND THEY THAT TURN MANY TO RIGHTEOUSNESS
AS THE STARS FOREVER AND EVER.

[1] *State of German Literature.*

IV

VICTOR HUGO, THE MAN OF LETTERS

Yes, a society that admits misery, a humanity that admits war, seems to me an inferior society and a debased humanity; it is a higher society and a more elevated humanity at which I am aiming, — a society without kings, a humanity without barriers.

I want to universalize property, not to abolish it; I would suppress parasitism; I want to see every man a proprietor and no man a master. This is my idea of true social economy. The goal may be far distant, but is that a reason for not striving to advance toward it?

Letter to Lamartine.

Have faith, then; and let us realize our equality as citizens, our fraternity as men, our liberty in intellectual power. Let us love not only those who love us, but those who love us not. Let us learn to wish to benefit all men. Then everything will be changed; truth will reveal itself, the beautiful will arise, the supreme law will be fulfilled, and the world shall enter upon a perpetual *fête* day. I say, therefore, have faith.

Speech to Workingmen's Congress.

VICTOR HUGO

IV

VICTOR HUGO, THE MAN OF LETTERS

" THIS century of ours was but two years old, the Sparta of the Republic was giving place to the Rome of the Empire, and Bonaparte the First Consul was developing into Napoleon the Emperor, when, at Besançon, there came into the world a child of mingled Breton and Lorraine blood, who was colorless, sightless, voiceless, and so poor a weakling that all despaired of him except his mother. . . . That child, whose name Life appeared to be erasing from its book, and whose short day of existence seemed destined to pass into night with never a morrow — that child am I." [1]

With this bit of autobiography Victor Hugo stands before us. When he was born Fichte the philosopher had just made his home in Berlin, and had twelve years more of heroic

---

[1] Quoted in Marzials's *Life*, p. 13.

work to do; Napoleon the First, as he tells us, was just setting out on that career of usurpation and conquest which was hastening to its close when Fichte lay dying.

Besançon is in the east of France, a little north of the railway route by which travelers are wont to cross the Jura from Pontarlier to Berne; it is an old Roman city — in Cæsar's day known as Vesontio — and it was the capital of the tribe of the Seguani, of whose exploits that warlike historian tells us. Extensive Roman ruins are visible there to-day — a triumphal arch, a theatre, and an amphitheatre. Not much place, however, had these august surroundings in the life of this infant; for Besançon was for his household a camp rather than a home. His father, Joseph Leopold Sigisbert Hugo, was an officer of the French army, and at the time of Victor's birth was about twenty-nine years old. He had apparently volunteered in the army of the Revolution; promotions were rapid in that time; in 1793 he was a captain in the Revolutionary forces, and was devoting his energies to the suppression of that revolt of the royalists in La Vendée, which Victor Hugo has so vividly pictured in "Ninety-Three," and

Balzac in " The Chouans." Doubtless Sigisbert Hugo was a good enough Republican,
and though he afterward followed the fortunes of Napoleon, it was because military
passion was stronger in him than political
conviction. The poet's mother was the daughter of a royalist of La Vendée; doubtless the
acquaintance was made while Sigisbert Hugo
was soldiering in that province; the fierce
antipathy of the Reds and the Blues could
not keep the young people apart, and after
Hugo returned to Paris and was established
in the war office, the maiden's father conducted her thither and they were married, in
1796. But now, with Napoleon at the head
of the army, a soldier's life was not likely
to be a stationary one, and Sigisbert Hugo
with his wife and babes was constantly on the
march. This was what brought him, at the
head of his battalion, to Besançon in February,
1802, where his third son, Victor Marie, was
born. The French fashion of giving girls'
names to boys seems to have been in vogue
in that neighborhood. Some of Mr. Stanley
Weyman's boys are represented as rebelling
against it; the difficulty is that long before
the bearer of the name has a chance to rebel

the mischief is past mending. Little Victor
Marie Hugo was consulted neither about
name nor local habitation ; puny as he was,
before he was six weeks old he must fall in
and march, — an infant in arms, indeed, —
first to Marseilles and then to Corsica and
Elba, the mother following, as long as she
could, the rapidly moving column to which
the father was attached.

There were three years of this camp life
for little Victor.   To an ordinary child they
would have signified little, but to one ex-
ceptionally precocious and by nature highly
imaginative they probably meant much.   Dr.
Bushnell tells us that more is done to affect
the character of children before they learn to
talk than after; that this is their " impres-
sional and plastic age; " that " whatever is
impressed or inserted here, at this early point,
must be profoundly seminal as regards all
the future developments of the character." [1]
If anything like this is true, the surroundings
of this little child for the first three years
must have left their impression on his character.   The emotional nature was, no doubt,
sufficiently stimulated in these experiences;

[1] *Christian Nurture*, pp. 238, 239.

if the character thus nurtured should in after years manifest rather more of passionate intensity than of philosophic calm there would be honest cause for it. The child whose home is in a camp and who catches daily from the face and from the lips of his mother her anxiety for the father whose life is often exposed to mortal peril, has begun his life in a kind of school which we should not choose for all our children. In one of his earlier poems Victor tells us how his cradle was sometimes rocked upon the head of a bass drum, and how he had learned in his childhood to drink water brought from the brook in a soldier's helmet, and how his covering in his sleep had sometimes been a tattered battle-flag.

In 1805, that portion of the army to which Sigisbert Hugo was attached was ordered to Italy, and the mother, with her three little boys, was compelled to return to Paris. Here for two years they dwelt, and here the child's education was begun. There was much flitting, after this, back and forth, to Italy and Spain, and a great deal of experience was accumulated during the first ten years of the lad's life ; but for the greater part of the time the mother and her sons lived in Paris, her husband away at the wars. These extended separations boded no good to the family ; the result was the estrangement and the permanent separation of the father and mother. Some of the biographers ascribe this to political differences, — the mother being a devotee of the old régime, while the father was a worshiper of Napoleon; but this is not, probably, the whole story. At all events the mother finds herself charged with the sole care of her three boys ; in the direction of their education the father appears to have reserved some rights, but she is mainly responsible.

A rather queer mixture of social and moral influences it was that encompassed this eager and impressionable boy. His mother, as we have seen, was an ardent champion of the Bourbon dynasty, but the theological outfit which usually went with that type of politics she wholly lacked ; instead of being a loyal Catholic she was a free-thinker after Voltaire's own heart ; she would not permit her sons at school to take part in the mass ; she encouraged them to read Voltaire and Rousseau and Diderot. Madame Sigisbert Hugo was a woman of much strength of character, and of some tender and passionate loyalty,

but the religious side of her nature had never
been developed.

Victor's first teacher, M. Larivière, was an
unfrocked priest who had married his cook;
it does not appear probable that his influence
over the child's mind could have been strin-
gent in the repression of liberal tendencies.
In his later years Hugo conceived that his
early education had been of an extremely conservative type; to that fact he ascribed the
monarchical and religious spirit of his earlier
works. But this is certainly unfair to those
who had the care of him. It is not, indeed,
easy to understand just how he came by such
opinions as he found himself in possession of in
the days of his adolescence. His royalisms we
may impute to his mother; his religious faith
must have been of more spontaneous growth.
Perhaps there was a natural religiousness in
him, which readily responded to the deeper
verities of the spirit. In one of his poems,
published when he was in exile at Guernsey,
he describes an experience in "The Feuillan-
tines" — their first home in Paris — where he
and his two little brothers, left to themselves
for an afternoon, found in an old convent loft
a book which was on a shelf beyond their
reach : —

"One day we tried until we reached the great black book.
How 't was I cannot say that we the treasure took,
But that a Bible 't was, this I remember well.

"Just like a censer's smell was the old book's perfume.
Rejoiced, at once we sought the corner of the room ;
We found it full of prints, what glory and delight !

"We spread our precious prize wide open on our knees,
And the first words we read did so our fancy please
That we went reading on, our games forgotten quite.

"Thus we three read and read, till out the morning ran,
Joseph, Ruth, Boaz, and the Good Samaritan ;
And ever better pleased, at eve, too, read it oft.

" As children who have made some bird of heaven their prize,
Laughing, each other call, with joyous wondering eyes,
To find beneath their hands how smooth its down and soft."

This is probably a credible reminiscence, and
it shows that his mind was not, at this time,
being forced into the moulds of traditionalism.
In fact, we may very well hesitate, upon such
evidence as his own writings furnish us, to accept Victor Hugo's estimate either of his early
conservatism or his later radicalism.   He was
never such a bigot as he charges himself with
being, nor was he ever such an agnostic as he
tries to make out.   Toward institutional religion there was some change in his attitude ;
toward the greater truths of spiritual religion

none worth emphasizing. The home of the mother and her three little boys in Paris was in a large house once attached to a convent, and connected with a great uncultivated garden that was half a park ; here the lads had happy times together, and there is a little girl of the neighborhood, Adèle Foucher, who is their constant playfellow. The elder of the boys, Abel, goes to the Lycée, a public school not far away ; the two younger, Eugène and Victor, are under the care of that ex-priest, M. Larivière. In Victor's twelfth year the two are removed by the father's request to the Pension Cordier et Decotte, to be prepared for the Polytechnic School, which is the training place for military service, especially for military engineering. Here they remain three years.

Belying the auguries of his feeble infancy, Victor grew up to be a stout and vigorous boy, full of life and enterprise, fond of fun and not averse to fighting. " The future king of men," says M. Marzials, " began by being king of boys. He and his brother led rival parties among their school companions, and exercised most despotic rule." [1]

His activity was not, however, all muscular.

[1] *Life of Victor Hugo*, p. 13.

He left this school in his sixteenth year, but not before he had done a prodigious amount of writing, — verse-making mainly, some of which had already won him considerable distinction. Genius is a term almost copious enough for the use of a reporter ; just what it connotes we may not confidently say, but we can hardly go amiss in ascribing it to this youth. Imagination of the most fecund sort he certainly possessed, and into his young life had been poured such a wealth of experience as falls to the lot of few. He had feasted his young eyes on the beauty of Italy, he had reveled amid the romantic scenes of Spain ; he knew very intimately the meaning of war ; the throes of the Napoleonic struggle, the passionate joy of France over the great victories, her piteous prostration when the desperate game was played out — all of this had entered into his boyish experience, and smitten, with might, on all the chords of life. Verse was the only vent for this surging emotion. His father had forbidden him to make verses ; that was like forbidding a rivulet to run down hill. I do not find that he neglected his other work in school ; he took high rank in mathematics and in physics, but the amount of literary production is almost incredible. " During the three years which he spent at the Pension De-cotte," says Madame Hugo, " he wrote verses of every possible kind, — odes, satires, epistles, poems, tragedies, elegies, idyls, imitations of Ossian, translations of Virgil, of Lucian, of Ansonius, of Martial, songs, fables, tales, epi-grams, madrigals, logographs, acrostics, cha-rades, rebuses, impromptus. He even wrote a comic opera." Mr. Marzials quotes a dictum of Théophile Gautier to the effect that a poet ought to exercise his 'prentice hand on at least fifty thousand lines of verse before ever writ-ing anything for publication, and expresses the opinion that Victor Hugo must have come up to this demand.[1]

When he was fifteen the French Academy proposed this subject for a prize poem : " The Happiness that Study can procure in Every Situation of Life." A promising theme for a poet, verily ! The Immortals must have evolved it from a studious perusal of the En-cyclopædia. As well expect one to wax ima-ginative and lyrical over the multiplication table or a book of logarithms. But that was what you had to write about, A. D. 1817, if

[1] *Life of Victor Hugo*, p. 36.

you wished to gain the prize of the French Academy. Victor Hugo was equal to making poetry out of almost anything, and he plunged into the contest with no misgivings. How to get it before that august body when written was the problem. A friendly usher of the school who was in the secret took the boys out walking, led them to the fountain in front of the Institute, and while the rest of them were watching the fishes, ran with Victor into the office of the secretary, dropped the manuscript there, and ran away again. It was an amazing presumption, no doubt, for a boy of fifteen to compete for the poetical prize of the French Academy; but the amazing fact is that, although he did not win the prize, — which was split, that year, between M. Lebrun, the author of " Marie Stuart," and Saintine, the author of " Picciola," — he was accredited an " honorable mention," his name being the ninth on the list. Doubtless the vow which the lad had registered in his copy book the year before, " I will be Chateaubriand or nothing," seemed even to himself a little less audacious after this.

From this hour he goes steadily forward, never slackening his rate of production. One of the elements of genius he certainly possesses, capacity for sustained, intense, concentrated effort. His calling is as clear to him as Michelangelo's was at the same age ; no École Polytechnique for him; not a military engineer by any means ; the pen is his tool, and it will be mightier in his hand than the sword.

All this is in sharp opposition to his father's will ; therefore the allowance is cut off and Victor is left to struggle for bread. For the next four years his pen flies swiftly. His elder brother Abel has also become a writer, and the two youths launch a semi-monthly journal named the " Conservateur Littéraire." The title conveys the purpose of the periodical ; it is to gather up and express the most conservative ideas in literature and art ; the youth who is to stand forth a few years later as the champion of romanticism in literature now holds a brief for the classicists. The amount of his contribution to this periodical was enormous. Poetry of many kinds, historical sketches, political essays, stories, literary criticism, discussions of painting and the drama, — it is remarkable how many things the youth attempts and with what cleverness they are done. The magazine was maintained for a year and a half and formed three volumes, — two thirds of it all by Victor. In 1822 a volume of odes and poems was gathered out of this periodical and published, the first volume from his pen.

The financial success of this journal had not been brilliant; in the fight for life through all those days there was never a moment's truce. Seven hundred francs — one hundred and forty dollars — was the extent of one year's income; out of that he saved enough to buy a dress coat with gilt buttons, and he often had a little money to lend. What rigid economy all this involved may be guessed at by some of us. In " Les Misérables," the experiences of Marius, just setting out as a young littérateur, are undoubtedly autobiographical.

" Life became severe for Marius : eating his clothes and his watch was nothing, but he also went through that indescribable course which is called ' roughing it.' This is a horrible thing which contains days without bread, nights without sleep, evenings without candle, a house without a fire, weeks without work, a future without hope, a threadbare

coat, an old hat at which the girls laugh, the
door which you find locked at night because
you have not paid your rent, the insolence of
the porter and the eating-house keeper, the
grins of neighbors, humiliations, dignity trampled under foot, any kind of work accepted,
disgust, bitterness, and desperation. Marius
learned how all this is devoured, and how it
is often the only thing that a man has to eat.
At that moment of life when a man requires
pride because he requires love, he felt himself
derided because he was meanly dressed and
ridiculous because he was poor. At the age
when youth swells the heart with an imperial
pride, he looked down more than once at his
worn-out boots and knew the unjust shame
and burning blushes of wretchedness. It is
an admirable and terrible trial from which the
weak come forth infamous and the strong
sublime. It is the crucible into which destiny
throws a man whenever it wishes to have a
scoundrel or a demigod." [1]

In the midst of this struggle with poverty
the death of his mother brings his first deep
sorrow. It was not, indeed, until his home
was broken up that his circumstances became

[1] *Les Misérables :* Marius, v. 1.

desperate. Through all this bitter experience he had been cherishing a tender regard for the little girl who used to play with him in the old garden ; they had not been permitted to meet very often, but the childish attachment strengthened with their years, and on the death of his mother Victor sought her, and their common sorrow melted the hearts of her obdurate parents, so that their betrothal was sanctioned, and there was nothing between them and home but the winning of a livelihood. For that they had not long to wait. The first edition of his Odes brought him quick recognition and something more; he realized from the sale quite a substantial sum of money, and the king, Louis XVIII. granted him from the privy purse a pension of one thousand francs. Thus Victor is able, in his twenty-first year, to claim his Adèle. They were married at St. Sulpice, and found their first home with the parents of the bride at Chantilly.

In 1823, not long after his marriage, appeared his first novel, " Han d'Islande," a somewhat lurid and ghastly tale, the production, Hugo himself said long afterward, " of a young man, of a very young man. One feels in reading it that the child who wrote it had as yet no experience of things, of men, or of ideas, and that he sought to divine them all." Along with this sensational story were published one or two other collections of odes and ballads, and the star of the poet began to ascend. The king increased the poet's pension on account of some pretty things which Victor had said about him, and the fortunes of the young housekeepers were flourishing.

With the exception of " Han d'Islande," Hugo's work had kept closely to classical models. In his preface to the volume entitled " Nouvelles Odes," which appeared in March, 1824, he disclaims partisanship in the quarrel between the classicists and romanticists, but pretty clearly indicates his own adherence to the literary methods of Boïleau and Racine. In 1827, when he was twenty-five years of age, a sudden change came over the spirit of his dream. The youth who had been a stickler for the nice proprieties and conventional elegancies of the old French masters struck out in a most daring way into a wholly new style. A drama, " Cromwell," was the first venture in this new form. The preface to this play announced his new theory of dramatic poetry and opened a battle that was not fought out for many a day.

The eighteenth century had stiffened and petrified poetry. You know how precise and formal much of our English verse of that period was; how Pope, and Thomson, and Collins, and Young, and Akenside measured it out and trussed it up and starched it and ironed it and counted its ruffles and its gussets, and combed its hair, and made it sit down on a stool in the corner and fold its hands and be good; the propriety of the poor muse under all these nurses and schoolmasters and drill masters was something melancholy.

From this dreary conventionalism English poetry freed itself much earlier than French; indeed the literary formalities were never quite so rigid north of the channel, and we had our own splendid background of Chaucer and Spenser, and Ben Jonson and Shakespeare, in whose presence literary art could not long be mummified; so that in the early part of our century Wordsworth and Scott and Shelley and Byron and Keats and Coleridge led poesy out into the English fields and woods and set her free. But the day of deliverance

came later in France, — chiefly, perhaps, because there was an Academy over there; and
a literary Academy is a great force for keeping literature to the proprieties, but not for
informing it with new life. Deliverance came,
at length, and it was Victor Hugo who stood
forth as the protagonist in this emancipation.
" Dramatic verse," he maintained in the preface to his " Cromwell," " should be free,
frank, direct, sufficiently outspoken to say
everything without prudery or affectation,
able to pass by natural transition from the
comic to the tragic, from the sublime to the
grotesque, by terms matter-of-fact and practical, at once artistic and inspired, profound
and full of surprises, large and true."

Such was the doctrine, good and wholesome, beyond doubt; and the practice, so far
as Hugo was concerned, was made to correspond. " Cromwell" was far too long to be
acted, but after a while appeared another play,
" Hernani; " a venturesome manager undertook to stage it and the battle was on. A
large number of the younger *littérateurs*,
students and artists, partisans of the new mode
in art and letters, determined that the play
should succeed, while the great body of the

respectable and conservative writers and critics and players meant that it should be driven from the stage. It was a motley crowd of the young romanticists that gathered for the first night of " Hernani." You could hardly call them the *sans-culottes* of the literary revolution, for they had on clothes enough, such as they were ; in Madame Hugo's words, "strange, uncouth, bearded, long-haired, dressed in every manner except according to the existing fashion, in loose jerkins, in Spanish cloaks, in Robespierre waistcoats, in Henry III. bonnets, having every century upon their shoulders and heads." Evidently these young men were ready to go far in their protest against conventionalities. They gained entrance in a body to the theatre at two o'clock in the afternoon, to hold the seats against the onrush of their adversaries; they brought with them sausages, ham, chocolate, and bread, and made a picnic of it. When the hour of seven came and the performance began, bedlam was let loose. All the evening the house was in an uproar. The beauties of the play, and they were not wanting, were applauded to the echo by partisans of the new mode ; its grotesque and unconventional features were

greeted with hisses and hootings by the other
side. So it went on for forty-five nights, with
roars of laughter and tumults of applause,
with jeers and cheers. " Each performance,"
says Madame Hugo, " became an indescribable
tumult. The boxes sneered and tittered, the
stalls whistled; it became a fashionable pas-
time to go and laugh at ' Hernani.' Every one
protested after his manner and according to his
individual nature. Some, as not being able to
bear to look at such a piece, turned their backs
to the performance ; others declared aloud
that they could stand it no longer and went
out in the middle of the acts, banging the
doors of their boxes as they went. The more
peaceable ostentatiously spread out and read
their newspapers."

What was it all about? It was simply the
question whether dramatic poetry should con-
form to the rules and models of the French
classic drama, or whether it might wear a looser
costume and travel at a freer gait. One would
say that there might have been a little more
toleration on both sides, but that was not
their way. Frenchmen say that the English
take their pleasures sadly ; certain it is that
the French contend for their æsthetic prefer-

ences furiously. Art is the religion of many of
them ; and human nature can be just as secta-
rian and just as intolerant in art as in religion.
There was, no doubt, a bigoted orthodoxy of
literary art in those days which had determined
that no novelties of expression should be al-
lowed, and this petty tyranny had to be defied
and overthrown. This was the movement of
which Victor Hugo was the leader. On the
whole it won an important victory for art, but
victories won in such passionate contests are
always costly ; much that was precious in the
old literature these fierce reformers despised
and trampled under their feet, and that was
not good for them nor for their art. The new
literature, under Hugo's championship, won
its battle to this extent, — it gained the right
to exist, and the heresy of the first quarter of
the century became the orthodoxy of the second. It did not, however, overthrow or exter-
minate the classic literature ; that still abides
in honor and power.

Not only into dramatic poetry, but into lyrical as well, the same courageous innovations
were carried ; the volumes of verse that appeared, one after another, from Hugo's pen,
struck another and a distinctly fresher note.

It seems to be admitted that the verse of Victor Hugo touches the high-water mark of literary art in France. Of this none can speak confidently but those who know French well enough to think in it. Translations of poetry, in their best estate, are but dim images of the original beauty. The perfection of the poem consists not only in the idea, but especially in the form, — in the music of the line, in the collocation of the words, in sweet suggestions that come through assonance as well as rhythm and rhyme, in delicate shadings of meaning which can no more be transferred from language to language than one woman's smile can be imitated by another woman. It is only the skeleton of a poem which we get in the best translation ; yet the versions which are presented to us by Hugo's translators indicate something of the wealth of his imagination. Those who have a right to speak tell us that he was a master of melody; the claim is even made for him that he is the greatest lyric poet of all literature.

His first signal triumph as a novelist was won by his " Nôtre Dame de Paris," published in 1831, when he was twenty-nine years old, — a magnificent historical romance, bringing

back in a series of sketches and characteriza-
tions the life of the fifteenth century. With
the publication of this book Victor Hugo
takes a place of honor and eminence. At this
early age he is certainly among the most distinguished men of letters in the world. A
band of the most loyal admirers are chanting
his praises. He has a happy home, and his
three children, Léopoldine, Charles François,
Victor, are the delight of his heart.

Most of his literary production during the
ten years that follow is poetic, and the strain
is tinged with a certain melancholy. " Au-
tumn Leaves," " Songs of the Twilight,"
" Voices Within," " The Rays and the Shadows," — the titles of the books suggest the
pensive atmosphere of much of this work.
What the cause of this may be we but dimly
understand ; the disillusions which come with
success, one may fancy. The great prizes of
life are splendid, — until we have won them.
It was one who had gotten about all that man
can crave who cried : " Vanity of vanities, all
is vanity ! "

Possibly Hugo's soul was shadowed by the
clouds that hung over the nation. Poor
France had been through her Inferno just

before he was born, and it was by no means
clear that the Purgatorio of the Restoration,
through which she had been passing since the
downfall of Napoleon, was leading her to
Paradise. Unhappy France ! In the long
night of mediævalism she had wandered with
the rest in the glooms of the wilderness, and
in the massacre of St. Bartholomew she had
put out the light that might have guided her
to freedom and peace. The slaughter of a
hundred thousand such men as perished on
that fateful night is a crime for which it will
take some centuries to atone. The Revolution and the unrest which followed it were
the natural penalty of the extermination of
that element in the population which might
have led the nation forward in the paths of
peaceful progress. When the Revolution had
swept away the old régime, steady hands to
guide the people were wanting, and the man
on horseback seized his opportunity. When
his vast usurpations had brought down upon
France the inevitable retribution, the people,
in despair, called back the Bourbon princes,
and the reaction was accomplished.

When Louis XVIII. returned to Paris, Victor Hugo was a boy in school; his mother's

passionate loyalty found full expression, and
he shared her exultation. His earlier writings
are tinged with this sentiment; the king was
kind to the budding poet, and to speak truth,
he was a gracious and liberal ruler, the best
of the Bourbons, and always disposed to enlarge the bounds of freedom. But when, at
his death, Charles X. succeeded him, the
worst elements of Bourbon rule were again in
power, and the buried seeds of popular dis-
content quickly sprouted. Nor did the overthrow of this despot and the accession of
Louis Philippe greatly mend matters; it was
a weak and sordid rule; the popular fermen-
tation increased, and the Second Revolution
was gathering its forces. Through this period
Victor Hugo had been rapidly unlearning his
early lessons in politics and was becoming less
and less a worshiper of monarchy. When
Charles X. went out and Louis Philippe came
in, his word was: " What we require is a republic in fact and a monarchy in name." As
the time wore on and the monarchy in name
brought slight relief, he began to think that
the name might as well be dropped; so that
when the days of 'Forty-eight ushered in the
Second Revolution, it found him a convinced

Republican, yet of moderate views. He was a member of the constituent assembly by which the Republic was decreed, and his whole conduct through the earlier part of that turbulent period was full of dignity and wisdom. But the fierce outbreak of the more radical element again provoked a reaction, and the man on horseback was soon again in power. Against the brazen and conscienceless usurpations of Louis Napoleon, Victor Hugo fought with all his might. Something theatrical there is, no doubt, in his attitude through this final struggle; more than once he hurts the cause by his violence; many of his speeches may be fine rhetoric, but they are poor politics; they helped to deepen the popular distrust of the more radical Republicans and thus to clear the path for the usurper. Still there shines through it all the spirit of a great-hearted man to whom such abominable treachery and baseness as that by which the Third Napoleon climbed to the throne is a thing with which no compromise can be made, for which no excuses can be admitted; a thing which success only makes more hateful and damnable; a thing which must be resisted to the end and driven from the earth, if we mean that the earth shall be a fit place for men to live in. In all this hot and relentless wrath against this monumental usurper, Victor Hugo wins the admiration of every man of honor. Of course, when the *coup d'état* had fully succeeded, Paris was not a safe place for him. Whether a price was set upon his head by Louis Napoleon or not, it is certain that he was the last man whom that dictator wanted near his throne. For some days he was a fugitive, flitting from place to place. At last, with a forged passport and in disguise, he escaped to Brussels, whence, within a short time, he issued his terrific indictment of the usurper, " Napoleon the Little." In all literature we shall not find fiercer invective. The French language lends itself to purposes of this nature, — its rapier-like point and keenness of edge make it a telling weapon. No man ever wielded it more skillfully than Hugo ; these sentences flash and crackle and hiss in their intensity. It was a mighty testimony, and it was its truth that made it terrible. And although it seemed to pass almost unheeded, and France, caring more for peace than for honor, stifled her conscience for many a day, and suffered this usurper to lift her into a fool's paradise of false prosperity that he might plunge her into the abyss of dishonor and dismemberment, through all these years the lightnings of this insatiable invective never ceased smiting the foundations of that crumbling throne, nor its thunders from calling on the heavens for the retribution which, though it tarried long, came at length with terrible majesty.

The immediate result of the publication of the book was the expulsion of Hugo from Brussels; the Belgian government did not dare to harbor such a foe to the French emperor, and he was bidden to depart out of their coasts. So he took up his journey to the Isle of Jersey, one of the English islands in the channel, not far from the northern coast of France, on which, and on its sister island of Guernsey, for eighteen years, and until the fall of the Second Empire, in 1870, he made his home. He might have gone back earlier, but he would not go; under that detestable empire he would never live.

Here in this beautiful seclusion he endured as best he could the loneliness of exile; his time was all his own and his pen was in his hand; a large part of the work by which he

is best known was the fruit of this solitude.
Of his poems the volumes entitled "Chastise-
ments," "Contemplations," and "The Legends of the Centuries" were here produced ;
of his prose works, "Les Misérables," "The
Toilers of the Sea," and "The Man who
Laughs."

The volume entitled "Contemplations,"
however, though it was not published until
1856, contains much work which had been
done at an earlier day.   It was in 1843, nearly
ten years before his exile, that his eldest
daughter Léopoldine, who had been his most
intimate companion, was married to Charles
Vacquerie.   One of his most touching poems
is that in which he sends the light of his eyes
and the joy of his heart away to another
home : —

> " Love him who loves thee and with him be blest :
> Farewell ; his treasure be as thou art mine !
> Go, my blest child, to the new home, now thine,
> And make them happy, and leave us distrest.

> " We would fain keep ; they long for thee the while ;
> Daughter, wife, angel child, with duties cope
> Twofold ; leave us regret, and bring them hope ;
> Go forth with tears and enter with a smile! "

There is another touching lyric which imagines the loneliness that her departure will leave behind : —

> " To the fields what shall I say —
>   Witness of my hopeless woe ?
> With the stars' bright golden ray,
>   With the flowers, what shall I do ?
>
> . . . .
>
> " What, without thy fellowship
>   Do with day ? do with the skies ?
> With my kiss without thy lip ?
>   With my tears, without thine eyes ? "

But the imagined loneliness of this partial separation was a sweet sorrow compared with the overwhelming grief that was in store for him. Within a few months Léopoldine and her husband, out for an evening's sail upon the Seine, were overturned by a sudden wind, and both were drowned. It was the one tragedy of Hugo's life; for a long time it benumbed him; there was no music in him; the motive of life was gone. When at last he found his voice, how piteous is the cry !

> " When we our life together led
>   On the hillside, now long ago,
> Where waved the trees and waters sped,
>   Where the house hugged the wood below, —
>
> " She was ten years ; thrice ten was I ;
>   I was the universe to her ;
> How sweet the grass ; how clear the sky
>   Beneath the thick green woods of fir !

> " My lot she glad and happy made,
>   My labors light, and blue my sky ;
> When she ' My father !' to me said,
>   My full heart would ' My God !' reply.

> " I was so young when she was born
>   To shine upon my destiny ;
> She was the child of my glad morn,
>   The star of dawn that lit my sky."

Yet it is not a rebellious cry. There is one most pathetic song, in which he stands at her grave and lifts up his lamentation to the Infinite One above him, pouring out the deepest woe of his heart submissively yet pleadingly — begging that he may not be too severely judged if he cannot find comfort : —

> " I come to thee, O Lord, who art, I know,
>   O living God ! good, merciful, and kind ;
> I own that you alone know what you do ;
>   That men are reeds that tremble in the wind.

> " I say the tomb wherein the dead are shut
>   Opes on the heavenly hall ;
> And what we here for end of all things put
>   Is the first step of all.

> " To-day I who erst was as a mother weak
>   Crouch at your feet, before your open skies ;
> I feel a light on my dark sorrows break,
>   As on your worlds I look with juster eyes.

> " Lord, now I see the madness of the man
>   Who e'er to murmur dares ;

I cease from all reproach, I cease to ban,
But oh, permit me tears."

Without this volume of "Contemplations"
the world would never have known the depths
of Victor Hugo's nature.

I must hasten to give in the briefest form
a mere outline of the last years of this eventful life.

In September, 1870, after the battle of
Sedan had pulverized Napoleon le Petit, Victor Hugo hastened back to Paris. It was late
in the evening when he arrived, but his coming had been noised abroad, and a crowd was
waiting for him at the station. " Vive Victor
Hugo ! " they cried ; " but there were wounded
men in the train, and the shout was silenced,
to be taken up again," says the reporter, " outside the station, by thousands upon thousands
of throats, and to roll, like a great sea of accla-
mation, all along the way to Paul Meurice's
house. ' Never,' says M. Alphonse Daudet,
the novelist, — ' never can I forget the sight
as the carriage passed along the Rue Lafayette,
Victor Hugo standing up and being literally
borne along by the multitude.' " [1]

---

[1] Marzial's *Life of Victor Hugo*, p. 191.

It was a royal welcome, but troublous days
were these, and the poet's whole thought was
given to the rescue of his people.   The iron
ring of the German army was closing around
Paris.   By permission of the German king
a representative Assembly was chosen by the
French people, to meet in Bordeaux and deter-
mine what France should do in this exigency.
Would it continue the war or would it consent to be despoiled of Alsace and Lorraine?
Victor Hugo was elected to this Assembly.
His speeches were battle cries.   His heart was
stout for resistance.   The Assembly was full
of confusion ; no clear policy was presented ;
Hugo's speeches did not help to crystallize
opinion.   Suddenly he struck a note that
made hideous discord — not because it was a
false note, but because it was clear and true.
Garibaldi had been chosen to the Assembly
from Algiers, and there was a proposition to
annul that election.   Why ?   Because the
rural gentry, who were good Catholics, were
strong in the Assembly, and Garibaldi was
anti-clerical.   The proposition to throw out
Garibaldi roused Victor Hugo.   No power
in Europe, he said, had come to the defense
of France in this struggle.   " Not a king, not

a state, none, with one single exception. This man, what did he have? His sword. This sword had delivered one people. It might save another. He thought so; he came; he fought for us."[1] The Assembly was at once in an uproar. "Death to Victor Hugo! Death! Death!" shouted some of these excited Frenchmen. The insult was more than he could endure. Turning upon the mob that was yelling at him he shouted: "Three weeks ago you refused to listen to Garibaldi. To-day you refuse to listen to me. This is enough. I tender you my resignation."[2] It was written in a moment and handed to the president, and Victor Hugo walked out of the Assembly; not a dignified action assuredly, though a generous sentiment inspired it. It was no time for heroics, but rather for conciliatory speech and judicious action. Neither the mob that raged at the praise of Garibaldi, nor the orator who provoked and then resented their rage showed much capacity for statesmanship.

This practically ended his public service.

[1] *Victor Hugo, his Life and Works*, by Alfred Barbou, p. 150.
[2] *Ibid.* 151.

He was, indeed, once more elected to the Senate, and after the suppression of the Commune he exerted all his powers to secure clemency for the communards, but his active participation in public affairs from this time forward amounts to little.

His pen is as busy as ever. From his seventieth to his eighty-third year his production was larger than that of the entire lifetime of some men of renown. Not less than seventeen volumes were published during this period, among them his last great novel " Ninety-Three " and several volumes of verse, — two more volumes of " Legends of the Centuries," one entitled, " The Four Winds of the Spirit," and one — most charming of all — written for his grandchildren, " The Art of Being a Grandfather " (*L'Art d' Être Grandpère*). Into this beautiful book he gathered the late blooms of his affection for all that were left of his household. His wife had gone to her rest in 1868; his son Francis, in 1873; Charles died suddenly on the day of his resignation of the senatorship in Bordeaux; the widow of Charles, with her two children, Georges and Jeanne, made his household in the Rue de Clichy. It was a serene old age. As death drew near his spirit was at peace ; his hopes were bright for the life to come, and his optimism was clear and strong to the end. On May 22, 1885, his deliverance came.

The memorandum relating to his funeral, given to a friend some time before his death, said : " I give 50,000 francs to the poor. I wish to be taken to the grave in their hearse. I refuse the prayers of all churches. I ask for a prayer from every human soul. I believe in God."

On the morning of May 31, by order of the government, they carried his body up to the Arch of Triumph, and it lay there in state for one day in a coffin richly draped with black and silver and royal purple ; then it was carried to the grave as the poet had decreed in a pauper's hearse, but with splendid pomp, in a great procession and with such tributes of respect and reverence as France has rarely bestowed on her most illustrious dead.

As we seek now to gather up the results of this great life, what can we say of it? It has been made clear by this recital that we are not dealing with a perfect character. Victor Hugo's limitations are apparent. His central fault, no doubt, was his egotism, which was colossal. Mr. Marzials puts his finger on the great man's weakness : —

"The fact is, and one says it sadly, there was a strong element of theatricality about the man. Great as he was, he liked to appear greater. His statements about himself, his surroundings, the events in which he had himself taken part, bear often the same proportion to fact that the stage bears to real life. They lack the simplicity of truth. They are, in effect, false. There, the murder is out; and if there be any one who cannot esteem a character tainted with theatricality, why then he must leave Victor Hugo unhonored. But I, for one, shall not agree with him. Behind the actor in Victor was a man, and a great man, in his private life simple, genial, and kindly, and in his public life filled with passionate convictions for which he was prepared to battle and to suffer. In the essential heart of him he was genuine enough. The theatricality, the vainglory, were of the surface." [1]

Hugo is an artist whose pictures are mainly in black and white; neutral tints and soft grays are not much employed. He deals too

[1] *Life of Victor Hugo*, pp. 209, 210.

much in contrasts and superlatives ; he screams
too often.   There is, as Rober' Louis Stevenson has said, " an emphasis which is akin to
weakness, a strength that is a little epileptic."

Those who deny that art can have a moral
purpose must, of course, exclude Victor Hugo
from the ranks of the artists.   His art, if art
it was, was pretty nearly all moral purpose.
Divest his poems and his stories of the enthusiasm of humanity and there would be little
left of most of them.   His own definition of
art is pertinent just here : —

> " Art, 't is a glory, a delight ;
>   In the tempest it holds fire-flight ;
>   It irradiates the deep blue sky.
>   Art, splendor infinite,
>   On the brow of the People doth sit,
>   As a star in God's heaven most high.
>
> " Art, 't is Humanity's thought
>   Which shatters chains century-wrought !
>   Art, 't is the conqueror sweet !
>   Unto Art — each world river, each sea !
>   Slave-People, 't is Art makes free ;
>   Free-People, 't is Art makes great."

Of all his novels it is especially true that the
moral significance is their very substance.   In
" Notre Dame " the purpose is to show how
inevitable are the disasters which a foolish and

rigid superstition always entails; in "The Toilers" it is the bitter fight of man with the external forces that moves our hearts; in "The Man who Laughs" the brutality of English aristocracy comes in for a scourging; and in the greatest of all, " Les Misérables," the moral purpose is, as Mr. Stevenson explains it, " to awaken us a little, if it may be — for such awakenings are unpleasant — to the great cost of the society that we enjoy and profit by; to the labor and sweat of those who support the litter, civilization, in which we ourselves are so smoothly carried forward. People are all glad to shut their eyes, and it gives them a very simple pleasure to forget that our laws commit a million individual injustices to be once roughly just in the general; that the bread we eat and the quiet of the family and all that embellishes life and makes it worth having have to be purchased by death, — by the deaths of animals and the deaths of men wearied out with labor, and the deaths of those criminals called tyrants and revolutionaries, and the deaths of those revolutionaries called criminals.   It is to something of all this that Victor Hugo wishes to open men's eyes in ' Les Misérables,' and this moral lesson is worked out in masterly coincidence with the artistic effect." [1]

If I may venture to supplement Mr. Stevenson, I would say that the ethical effects of Victor Hugo are largely gained by exaggeration. Mr. Stevenson himself unconsciously abets him in this when he says that "our laws commit a million injustices to be once roughly just in the general." That, I should say, is a considerable overstatement. Hugo, like Dickens, though in a different way, understood the artistic value of overstatement— of caricature even. By greatly overdrawing some defect of a man's physiognomy you call attention to that defect. It must be admitted that Hugo's social pictures have this character. It is this that makes them effective; men's thoughts are sharply drawn to the oppressions of society, to the burdens and sufferings and wrongs of the unhappy. Yet the overstatement in its turn works mischief; a kind of sentimentalism is bred by it which vitiates philanthropy; men come to believe that all criminals are made criminals by society, and that the woes of the unhappy are purely the product of their environment. That senti-

---

[1] *Familiar Studies*, p. 42.

ment is just as fatal to all sound social recon-
struction as is the heartless selfishness which
it rises to denounce.   It is by the swinging of
the pendulum of popular thought from one
extreme to the other that time is marked and
progress is made.   But whatever the exaggeration may be, the motive of this work of
Hugo's is the highest, and it is by the motive,
after all, that a man must be judged.

Hugo thought himself in religion a great
heretic ; here also, as I have said, he greatly
exaggerated.   What he said about the church
in those words I just quoted is inspired, of
course, by the only kind of ecclesiasticism with
which he was familiar.   After all, he is by his
own frank confession a man of deep religious
convictions.   His belief in God and immortality was not an esoteric theory ; it was constantly avowed ; some of his most beautiful
poems express in glowing words this vital
faith.   Thomas à Kempis himself could not
confess his dependence on God more humbly
that Hugo has confessed it in his poem, "Believe, but not in Ourselves."

> "God only great, the humble flowrets name ;
> And only true, the mighty floods proclaim ;
> And only good, winds tell from spot to spot.
> O man, let idle vaunts deceive you not.

Whence did you spring, to think that you can be
Better than God, who made the stars and sea,
And who awakes you when your rest is done,
With that prodigious smile of love, the sun ? " [1]

In that beautiful little melody " The Grave
and the Rose " how sweetly he sings the un-
dying hope : —

> " The Grave said to the Rose
>   ' What of the dews of dawn,
> Love's flower, what end is theirs ? '
>   ' And what of spirits flown, —
> The souls, whereon doth close
>   The tomb's mouth unawares ? '
> The Rose said to the Grave.
>
> The Rose said, ' In the shade
>   From the dawn's tears is made
> A perfume sweet and strange
>   Amber and honey-sweet.'
> ' And all the spirits fleet
>   Do suffer a sky-change,
> More strangely than the dew,
>   To God's own angels new,'
> The Grave said to the Rose."

Was Victor Hugo a Christian ? Not by
ordinary ecclesiastical definition. Probably
if you had asked him to accept any credal
statement about Jesus the Christ he would

[1] *Poems*, in three volumes : Estes & Lauriat, ii. 90.

have refused. But how deep and tender was his reverence for the Man of Sorrows; how profound his recognition of the mighty meaning of the self-sacrifice of the Son of Man, no one who reads his books needs to be told. Is not his good Bishop Bienvenu meant to be a copy of that great Original? Can any one forget that scene of the sinking ship in " The Man who Laughs," or the death-bed testimony of Jean Valjean?

" All at once he rose — such return of strength is at times a sequel of the death agony. He walked with a firm step to the wall, thrust aside Marius and the doctor, who wished to help him, detached from the wall the small copper crucifix hanging on it, returned to his seat with the vigor of full health, and said, as he laid the crucifix on the table, ' There is the *Great Martyr.* ' " [1]

These lines of his, also, written at the foot of a crucifix, how could one who found it in his heart to write them have ever imagined that his place was outside the great brotherhood of Christian believers?

" All ye that weep, come unto One who weeps ;
All ye who suffer, come to One who cures ;

[1] *Jean Valjean,* ix. v.

All trembling hearts be still ; He pity keeps ;
All passers-by, oh, tarry ; He endures ! " [1]

The one thing that Jesus Christ brought to earth, a great critic has said, was the enthusiasm of humanity. With that passion the soul of Victor Hugo was fully dowered, and he knew whence it came and reverently confessed Him.

No better words than his own can close this imperfect estimate : —

" The human race for four hundred years has made no step that was not decisive. We enter the great ages. The sixteenth century was the century of painters ; the seventeenth the century of writers ; the eighteenth the century of philosophers ; the nineteenth the century of apostles and prophets. To suffice for the nineteenth century one must paint as in the sixteenth, write as in the seventeenth, philosophize as in the eighteenth ; one must also possess . . . that fervid religious love for humanity which constitutes apostleship and which makes man clearly discern the future. In the twentieth century war will be dead, the scaffold will be dead, hatred will be dead, royalty will be dead, frontier bounda-

[1] *Poems*, in three volumes, ii. 85.

ries will be dead, dogmas will be dead ; man will live. He will possess something higher than all these, — a great country, the whole earth, and a great hope, the whole heaven." [1]

[1] *Victor Hugo,* by Alfred Barbou : Shaw's Translation, p. 191.

V

RICHARD WAGNER, THE MUSICIAN

Just as our master said of Beethoven's grand art that it had rescued the human soul from deep degradation, so no artist after him has presented this supreme and present spirit of our nation as sanctified and strengthened by Christianity, purer and clearer than he who had already confessed in early years that he could not understand the spirit of Christianity otherwise than as love. With " Parsifal " he has created for us a new period of development which is to lead us deeper into our own hearts and to a purer humanity. — *Louis Nohl.*

The transcendent beauty of the modern drama is lent by the ethical idea of salvation through the love of pure woman — a salvation of which no one can be in doubt when Tannhäuser sinks lifeless beside the bier of the atoning saint, and Venus's cries of woe are swallowed up by the pious canticle of the returning pilgrims. — *H. E. Krehbiel.*

WILHELM RICHARD WAGNER

RICHARD WAGNER, THE MUSICIAN

RICHARD WAGNER was born in Leipsic, May 22, 1813. That was a year before Fichte died in Berlin. Victor Hugo was then a boy of eleven, at school in Paris. Three of our Witnesses of the Light were thus alive together on the earth in this year 1813. Richard Wagner's death occurred in Venice, February 13, 1883 ; three months more would have carried him to his seventieth birthday. Between these dates are crowded a lifetime of tremendous work and many vicissitudes of fortune. Through the whole gamut of social condition — from gloomiest penury to sunniest prosperity, from heart-breaking isolation to a popularity that was almost worship, — fortune conducted him. Surely he must have known by indubitable experience many of those struggles of the soul which he has sought to represent to us by means of his art.

His father was a man of the middle class, clerk of the courts when we first know him; probably it was his superior education and his knowledge of the French language which led Marshal Davoust to commit to him the reorganization and control of the police force during the French occupation of Leipsic.

This was just the time, however, when the Prussians were making that heroic attempt to throw off the French yoke to which Fichte so bravely incited them; and when Richard Wagner was six months old that terrible battle of Leipsic — the battle of the nations — occurred, in which the empire of Napoleon received its death wound, and the invader was driven back across the Rhine. Doubtless the baby in his cradle heard the cannonading of that fierce fight. From the carnage of that battlefield arose a pestilence, one of whose victims was Friedrich Wagner; and his widow with seven children, the eldest of whom was but fourteen, and the youngest this baby in the cradle, was left in very narrow circumstances, her only reliance being a small pension from the government. Nine months later the widow was married to Ludwig Geyer, an actor of some celebrity, a writer of suc-

cessful comedies, and a portrait painter, who
had been an old friend of the family. It is
scarcely to be wondered at that the mother
of seven children should have been willing to
accept the protection of a reputable man
who offered to assume her burdens; and it
must have been a loving woman to whom,
with such encumbrances, a sensible man was
willing to make such an offer. " Her brightness and amiability," says Mr. Finck, " appear to have made her especially congenial to
artists, and among those who occasionally
dropped in for a friendly chat with her was
not less a personage than Von Weber, the
creator of the opera ' Der Freischütz,' which
first aroused young Richard's musical instincts.
Throughout his life Richard Wagner referred
to his mother as ' mein lieber Mütterchen,'
and at the age of forty-three he told his
friend Praeger that he could not see a lighted
Christmas tree without thinking of the kind
woman, nor prevent the tears starting to his
eyes when he thought of the unceasing activity of that little creature for the comfort and
welfare of her children. Praeger is doubtless
right in suggesting that the exquisitely tender
strains in ' Siegfried,' in which the orchestra

accompanies the reference to Siegfried's mother, symbolize the love of Wagner for his own mother. ' I verily believe,' he says, ' that Richard Wagner never loved any one so deeply as his *lieber Mütterchen.* All his references to her, of his childhood, were of affection, amounting to idolatry. With that instinctive power of unreasoned yet unerring perception possessed by women, she from his childhood felt the gigantic brain power of the boy, and his love for her was not unmixed with gratitude for her tacit acknowledgment of his genius.' " [1]

It required, indeed, the divination of maternal love to recognize this genius, for Richard Wagner was no such prodigy as Michelangelo or Victor Hugo. He was a fairly bright boy, but he was by no means precocious, and music was not his first love, though he began taking lessons on the piano at an early age. No such stories of his musical childhood can be told as those with which we are familiar in the biographies of Beethoven and Mozart and Mendelssohn; even Max Müller, who was only an amateur, gave far clearer evidence in his early years of a

[1] Finck's *Wagner and his Works,* i. 11, 12.

musical vocation than Richard Wagner could
ever have exhibited.

The family removed to Dresden in his early
childhood, where his stepfather held a position
in the Court Theatre, with which also his elder
brother and sister were connected. From his
childhood he was thus at home upon the stage.
The stepfather seems to have been fond of the
lad and might have helped to shape his career,
but in Richard's seventh year he died, and the
mother, with an addition to her brood, was the
second time a widow. "Shortly before his
death," Wagner writes, "I had mastered the
'Yungferm Kranz,' from 'Der Freischütz,' at
that time a novelty, on the piano. The day
before he died I had to play it to him in the
next room; after I had finished I heard him
say to my mother in his weak voice : 'Should
he have a talent for music?' The day after
my stepfather died my mother came into the
nursery and said something for him to every
child. To me she said, 'Of you he wanted to
make something.' I remember," Wagner
adds, "that for a long time I had an idea that
something might become of me."

Although the child was only seven years
old at the time, the impression made on his

mind by these two memorable sayings was undoubtedly permanent and powerful. No man
can tell how much may result from suggestions
of this sort, implanted at the right moment
in a sensitive soul.

At nine he went to school, but his masters
thought him an indifferent pupil. He would
not apply himself to his regular tasks; his
mind was too discursive. With his piano
lessons he did not get on; he would not practice. Yet he learned sonatas, overtures, and
such like, by the ear, they said; perhaps he
always learned music that way, though when
he came, by and by, to need the knowledge
of theory and harmony he acquired that with
resolution and thoroughness; none of the
masters knows his musical grammar better
than Wagner.

We cannot believe that his school time was
wholly wasted, for before he was eleven he
knew Greek well enough to translate into the
German twelve books of the Odyssey, and
English well enough to undertake the rendering of one of Romeo's monologues into German verse. Shakespeare, whom he knew best
in German translations, was at this time of his
life his hero: he began to imitate him. " I

projected," he says, " a grand drama, a sort of compound of ' Hamlet ' and ' King Lear ; ' the plan was extremely grandiose ; forty-two persons died in the course of the piece and in developing the plot I found myself compelled to make most of them appear as ghosts, because otherwise there would have been no personages left to reappear in the last acts."

The boy was a poet; so much was clear; he reveled in the study of mythology, which awakened all the energies of his imaginative mind, and he began, at an early day, to write verses. On the death of a schoolmate the teacher called for rhymed tributes from the children of his class; the best was to be printed and Richard Wagner's was selected for the purpose. This was his first public venture into the field of poesy.

In his later life he himself recalled his first absence from home. It was on the occasion of a visit to his uncle Geyer, at Eisleben, the birthplace of Luther, who was one of the heroes of his youth. "My family," he said, " had been among the stanchest Lutherans for generations. What attracted me most in the great Reformer's character was his dauntless energy and fearlessness. Since then

I have often ruminated on the true instinct of childhood, for I, had I not to preach a new gospel of Art? Had I not also to bear every insult in its defense, and had I not too said, 'Here I stand; God help me! I cannot do otherwise.' " Here is the consecrated purpose which makes this life significant to us. In some true sense it may be said that the same spirit which animated Luther burned in the heart of Wagner, — fidelity to the highest that he knew; readiness to suffer the loss of all things rather than be false to his ideals. It is interesting to find the boy Wagner kindling his torch at the great Reformer's fire.

Wagner's first musical awakening seems to have been under the baton of Von Weber; he tells of the awe with which he drew his little sister to the window as Weber went by to look upon the greatest man in the world. But the impression was not lasting, and it was not until the family returned from Dresden to Leipsic, when he was fifteen years old, that he first heard, at a Gewandhaus concert, the music of Beethoven. This made a profound impression upon him; the depths of his soul were stirred. Writing in after years, he puts into the mouth of another words which are probably autobiographical: "I knew not what I really was intended for. I only remember that I heard a symphony of Beethoven one evening. After that I fell sick of a fever; and when I recovered I was a musician." At once he began to think of composition. He must know musical theory and counterpoint, and he borrowed books and gave himself to study. The difficulties were greater far than he had imagined, but they only roused his energies; this was a task in which discouragement was not to be considered; all his powers were now concentrated; he borrowed from a circulating library a book on thorough bass, and pored over it in secret until he had absorbed the rudiments; before any one knew of the new direction of his mind he had composed a sonata, a quartette, and an aria. When at length the new ambition is confessed, a music teacher is employed by the family, but here again is apparent failure; Richard will not stick to his exercises in counterpoint; he wants to write overtures for grand opera, nothing less. It must be admitted that something like what the neurologists call megalomania is here indicated — a disposition to do big things or nothing. It is a symptom which

we observed also in Michelangelo and Victor
Hugo.   At sixteen he composed an overture,
an astonishing composition ; he says himself
laughingly that Beethoven's Ninth Symphony
was a simple and elementary thing by the side
of this marvelously complicated structure.
" It was the climax of my absurdities," says
Wagner.   However, he got the Leipsic orchestra to play it as an entr'acte, and it was
more successful than he wished, for it set the
orchestra and the audience all in a roar.   It
was a most useful lesson for the youth ; he
began to see that he was not above the need
of thorough study, and he was soon again at
work under a competent master and making
good use of his time.   Mozart and Beethoven
were the masters he followed ; for the latter
his admiration was little short of worship.   " I
am doubtful," writes one who was not his
friend, " whether there ever was a young musician more familiar with the work of Beethoven
than Wagner at eighteen.   He possessed most
of the master's overtures and large instru-
mental pieces in copies made by himself.   He
went to bed with the sonatas and rose again
with the quartettes.   He sang the songs and
whistled the concerti, for with pianoforte play-

ing he did not get on very well; in short it was a true *fervor Teutonicus* which, in its union with an intellect of scientific cultivation and unusual activity, promised to yield vigorous shoots." [1]

It must be evident that we have here something more than genius; we have learning, culture, of the highest and finest kind. A boy of eighteen who has made copies in his own handwriting of most of Beethoven's masterpieces — who has analyzed them and understands them — may be said to have a pretty fair musical education. Something more than native aptitude for music is in him; his memory is stored with a vast accumulation of musical lore.

He begins writing now in good earnest and produces a few symphonies and overtures that still live. At the age of twenty he was chorus-master of the theatre of Würzburg, a year later he was director of the theatre at Magdeburg, and here the low standards of the popular taste and the loose morality of his associates began to work considerable demoralization in him; the fermentations of adolescence were not yet past. An opera in

[1] Finck's *Wagner,* i. 31.

two acts, " Das Leibesverbot," an overture to Apel's play "Columbus," and other lesser things, came from his pen while here. His next halting-place was Königsberg, where Fichte found Kant, and where Wagner found his fate in the person of a young actress whom he married, thus consigning himself to an ill-assorted union with one who could never share the best part of his life. Here life gained such sweetening as can be given through the uses of adversity; for poverty was his comrade, and debt drove him at length away to Riga, where for a year he was music director, doing indefatigable work, and managing to save money enough to pay the debts left behind at Königsberg.

Now comes the first hegira of Richard Wagner. In the summer of 1839, with his wife, a big Newfoundland dog, a light purse and two acts of his opera "Rienzi" in his carpet-bag, he embarks at Pilau on a sailing vessel to London. Paris is his objective point; this opera of " Rienzi " will be finished when he arrives there, and he expects to have it performed at the Grand Opera. We shall all admit that this is an intention of the first magnitude; the self-confidence which it reveals is sublime. It is plain that the young man will not fail for lack of assurance. Yet it must also be admitted that Wagner was probably the only man in the world who at this time rightly estimated his own power; his expectation, preposterous as it seemed to everybody else, was in the highest degree rational. "Rienzi," the poorest of his operas, was not accepted at Paris, but, bad as it was, it was better than anything which was accepted there while he was living in Paris. It would have been a great loss to the world if Richard Wagner had been less sure of himself. It would be poor economy for Providence to give a man a big endowment of faculty and fail to give him assurance enough to get that faculty recognized.

It was on this stormy voyage through the Skagerack and the Cattegat that one precious trophy was secured. "The passage through the Norwegian fiords," he says, "made a wondrous impression on my fancy; the legend of the Flying Dutchman, as I heard it confirmed by the sailors, acquired a definite peculiar color which only my adventures at sea could have given it." Thus was lodged in his mind the germ of his second great opera.

His stay in Paris was prolonged for three years, and his life there was a series of bitter disappointments. He had great hopes of many things, but none of them was realized. He wrote his " Faust " overture, and the conductor of the Conservatoire orchestra partly promised to bring it out, but finally recalled his consent; he tried to write songs, but nobody would buy them; he sought a place as chorus singer in a small theatre, but they told him he could not sing. An extract from his diary shows the straits to which he was brought.

" I hope that the writing down of my prevailing moods, and the reflection springing from them, will afford me relief as tears do to a heart oppressed. Tears have come into my eyes unbidden at this moment; is it a proof of cowardice or of unhappiness to yield willingly to tears? A young German journeyman was here; he was in poor health, and I bade him come again for his breakfast. Minna took the occasion to tell me that she was about to send away our last pennies for bread. You poor woman — right you are ! our situation is a sad one; and if I reflect upon it I can foresee with certainty that the greatest conceivable misery is in store for us; an accident only can bring improvement, for an accident I must almost consider the contingency of being helped by others voluntarily and without any personal interest."

He had many friends who seemed to value his talents but who were too busy to give him any practical aid. Meyerbeer, Berlioz, Halévy, Scribe, Vieuxtemps, and the Germans, Laube and Heine, were all numbered among his acquaintances, but even with such endorsement as they could give him, Richard Wagner, in his twenty-eighth year, was nigh to starvation. At length a music publisher found him work to do reading proof and arranging popular melodies and operatic airs for the piano and other instruments, not excluding even the cornet. What work was this for the author of " Tannhäuser " and " Parsifal ! " But it gave him bread; it kept him, perhaps, from self-destruction, to which he confesses that he was tempted.

Yet this stay in Paris was not wasted time. What good stuff was in him this experience revealed, for it was in this time of testing that his ideals were clarified and his highest purposes confirmed. During these three years in

the French capital, he finished his "Rienzi,"
and wrote the "Flying Dutchman." Paris
had no use for any of this work; he began to
correspond with friends in Dresden and to his
great delight his " Rienzi " was accepted there.
In the spring of 1842 he turned his steps
homeward with a great wish to do something
for the art and the people of his native country.
"For the first time," he says, " I saw the
Rhine; with tears in my eyes, I, the poor
artist, swore allegiance to the German Father-
land."

" Rienzi," crude as it was, was brilliantly
successful both in Dresden and at Berlin;
" Der Fliegende Holländer," a far more poetical and original work, was much less favorably
received, simply because it was more poetical
and original. It is in this work that Wagner
first takes deep counsel with himself concerning his art. Instead of asking what is fashionable and popular, he simply asks what is
true and beautiful. He is beginning the same
fight in musical art in which Hugo enlisted in
behalf of a better method in literature; and
it is to be a long and bitter warfare. It is
romanticism against classicism, it is the new
theology against the old orthodoxy, it is liberal-

ism against conservatism, it is the age-long struggle of life to break through the crust of conventions and find new forms of fruitfulness and beauty. There is always something to say on both sides of this question; there is always good in the old to be conserved, and there is often much that is crude and flighty in the militant innovations; but even when it is true of the innovator, as it was of Wagner, that there is full recognition of value in the old forms, and only desire to supplement and vitalize them with fresh growths, a stupid conservatism often rages against this laudable endeavor and determines to crush out every suggestion of change.

This is the kind of antagonism which Wagner now finds confronting him, and to which, from this hour, he makes no concessions; hitherto he has yielded, somewhat, to the demands of fashion; now he has his own ideas of what good music is, and he will be true to his own conceptions.

He has, indeed, won recognition for his genius; nobody questions that he is a true musician, and the honorable position of Royal Conductor of the Dresden Opera is now granted him, which he holds for six years.

The fruit of this period is "Tannhäuser" and "Lohengrin," the first of which is here performed under his direction, and the second of which is compelled to wait for a long time before it sees the light.

The popular reception given to "Tannhäuser" seems to have been enthusiastic enough at the outset, but the critics would none of it. The press was bitterly hostile, for reasons which, at this distance, do not seem entirely adequate. There was great lack of hilarity, these gentlemen affirmed, in the story; the third act was particularly devoid of interest, and the failure of the artist to bring about a matrimonial alliance at the end between Tannhäuser and Elizabeth appeared to them inexcusable. The clear word of Robert Schumann, applauding the beauty of the opera, was a voice crying in the wilderness.

The temper of the times, as revealed in the onslaught upon "Tannhäuser," which banished it from the stage and entailed upon Wagner severe financial losses, embittered him, and drove him into the ranks of the revolutionaries. This was in 1845, the uprising of '48 and '49 was simmering, and Wagner began to feel that the day had come for a com-

plete social change. He did not think that
art could breathe in that stifling atmosphere;
a thunderstorm must clear the air. Two
pamphlets written during this period indicate
the vital relation between his passion for art
and his political ideas. The loftiness of his
aims must be confessed. He thought that the
theatre and the opera ought to do something
more for the people than merely to furnish
them with diversion; they ought to be in the
highest sense educational and inspirational.
The Emperor Joseph's maxim he prints in
large letters in one of these pamphlets, —
" The theatre should have no other object
than to assist in the refinement of taste and
morals." The suggestions of his pamphlet
on the national drama are radical enough; he
wants its management placed in the hands of
competent specialists; he wants dramatic and
musical schools established for the training
of artists; he wants the music of the churches
reformed at the same time, and the whole
administration of opera and theatre placed
under the authority of *the minister of public
worship.*

It was because the standards and aims of
the stage, on the musical side as well as on

the theatrical side, were so low, — because
the Philistinism of the period fought so bitterly against any elevation of its perform-
ances, that Wagner became a revolutionist.
In the uprising of the Dresden populace for
republicanism he fired rockets, rang alarm
bells, wrote pamphlets, made speeches; whether
he fought at the barricades is not certain, but
he stood on the watch-towers and welcomed
the reinforcements from the villages who came
in to assist the insurrectionists.

How much better off Wagner would have
been if the revolution had been successful I
cannot say; it is not so certain that the substitution of a commercial for a political feudalism would have greatly liberated art.   Indeed,
it is evident that Wagner's liberalism would
never have marched far with that of his com-
patriots; for when he came to think out his
scheme for the reorganization of society he
found that monarchy — a hereditary monarchy — was an essential element in it.
" Wagner," says Mr. Lidgey, " believed in
Kingship as the fundamental principle of government; but in this belief his desire for revolution was retrogressive, and coupled with a
strong qualification.   The king must be su-

preme, but he must rule, first, *directly*, secondly, *over a free people*. Wagner's ideal of life was the Family. In the family the father is head, his supremacy is unquestioned, all the other members render him implicit obedience. Why? Because all are united by the supreme bond of Love. Their actions are dictated by no selfish spirit, no self-interest mars the happy union; each member is free, and his obedience (which is dictated only by Love) to the head of the little community necessarily results in the mutual well-being, seeing that it is prompted by the one dominant feeling of community of interest."[1] The idyllic unworldliness of this political programme was not, probably, the kind of thing that most of the people of the barricades had set their hearts upon. It was the kingdom of heaven which he proposed to establish on earth, without waiting for any. The ideal is high enough. He wanted a free field for the human spirit; and with all that was visionary he clearly saw what none of us must fail to see, that no single section of human life can be reformed without the reformation of the whole; that art and literature and education and religion are all

---

[1] *Wagner,* by C. A. Lidgey, p. 82.

affected by the prevailing social and political conditions, and that the remedy for their ailments must spring from a freer and healthier life in the whole people.

This revolutionary uprising was quickly put down by Prussian bayonets, and in the spring of '49 Wagner was forced to flee, first to Weimar, where Liszt sheltered him for a little, and thence to Zurich, where for more than nine years he made his home.   It was not till 1861 that he was permitted to return to his own country.   His exile was less prolonged than that of Dante, but hardly less flagrantly unjust; for Richard Wagner was German to his finger-tips, and from revolutionaries of his type the throne had not much to fear.

I cannot follow his career through the vicissitudes of these memorable years.   Most of the time he was in great poverty, kept from starving by the kindness of his friends, chief of whom was Franz Liszt, between whom and Wagner a most noble and beautiful affection existed.   To the friendship of this magnanimous soul Wagner owed a debt unspeakable, and he was not unmindful of the obligation.

It was during these years of exile that he wrote " Tristan und Isolde," " Die Meister-

singer von Nürnberg," and a considerable portion of his great tetralogy, " The Nibelungen
Ring"; it was in Zurich also that he produced his important literary works, in which
he develops his ideas of art. In 1861, by
the intercession of friends, his political of-
fenses were pardoned, and he was permitted
after an absence of twelve years to return to
his native country. In 1864 the romantic
young King of Bavaria called him to his side
and undertook to be his munificent patron;
there were great plans for a new theatre at
Munich, and magnificent interpretations of
Wagner's chief works, but court intrigues and
violent popular opposition interrupted these
schemes, and Wagner threw himself upon the
generosity of the German people, hoping by
subscriptions and concerts to obtain the money
necessary for the erection of the theatre in
which his works could be adequately rendered
under his own direction. The beautiful old
city of Bayreuth was selected as the site of
this building, and after much tribulation the
building was completed, King Ludwig coming
to the rescue with a generous subvention.
Here his great tetralogy was finished and performed under his own direction ; the old city

became a Mecca to which pilgrimages from the whole world were made, and finally, his sacred drama " Parsifal " was written and solemnly celebrated, the consecration and crown of his life-work. On February 13, 1883, in his temporary home on the Grand Canal in Venice, his end suddenly came. His body was buried in the grounds of his own house at Bayreuth — Wahnfried; the ivy-covered grave is unmarked by carven slab or obelisk; if you wish to see his monument look about you; the city is forever identified with his name.

To estimate, in any adequate way, the services rendered to art by this great master would be a serious task. Of the technical questions involved I must not try to speak, further than to say that Wagner's conceptions of musical form are the development of ideas struck out by Beethoven and Von Weber and Schumann. From him we have gained a new definition of melody. It is not with him a dance tune, in which the phrases are rhythmically symmetrical; it flows on without pausing and returning upon itself. It is not Long Meter nor Hallelujah Meter, nor 8s and 7s, nor any of their combinations; it wanders at its own sweet will, and comes round to its cadences when it pleases. This feature of his composition was, perhaps, at the outset, as much of a stumbling-block to the ordinary listener as anything else in Wagner's music. Wagner maintains that the adherence to the dance measures characterizes the childhood of musical art. Melody, as he conceives it, is less artificial. It should produce upon the spirit of the listener an effect " like that which a beautiful forest produces, on a summer evening, upon a lonely wanderer, who has but just left the town, . . . and who listens ever more keenly as one who hears with new senses and becomes with every moment more distinctly conscious of endlessly varied voices that are abroad in the forest. New and various ones constantly join, — such as he never remembers to have heard before ; and as they multiply in numbers they increase in mysterious power. They grow louder and louder, and so many are the voices, the separate tunes, he hears, that the whole strong, clear-swelling music seems to him only the great forest melody that enchained him with awe at the beginning." [1] One needs to become accus-

[1] *Art Life and Theories of Richard Wagner*, translated by Edward L. Burlingame, p. 182.

tomed to Wagner's way of saying things, as to Carlyle's way, or Burne Jones's way; but when our minds are adjusted to his manner we find it most stimulating and refreshing.

The doctrine of the fellowship of the arts was one on which Wagner placed the strongest emphasis. In his music-dramas — for he would not call them operas — poetry, painting, action, and music must all be harmoniously blended.

The Italian opera of fifty years ago, as some of us can remember, had sunk into an abyss of artificial puerility. It was a conventional trapeze, on which musical artists performed for audiences who thought themselves too cultivated to go to the circus. The structure of the opera was to the last degree artificial; as a drama it was ludicrous; the action was subordinated in the most laughable ways to vocal exigencies; the poetry was drivel; the whole thing was a contrivance for the exhibition of the vocal powers of a few astonishing singers. As Voltaire said: "What is too silly for speech they sing." Wagner's first principle is that the poetry and the music must be organically united; that the poetry is not a set of wooden pegs on which musical draperies may be hung;

that the purpose of the music is simply to give adequate expression to the thought and feeling which the words contain. The poetry is first, out of this the melody must naturally spring. It was a strong way of putting it when Wagner used to liken poetry to a husband and music to a wife, observing at the same time that he did not believe in " woman's rights ; " maintaining that, in the music-drama, at any rate, the poetry should never be subordinated to the music. There may, however, be a deeper truth here than Wagner himself divined ; for the Christian doctrine, in which he so profoundly believed, that self-surrender is conquest and mastery, is revealed in the right relation of the sexes. The very subordination of the feminine music, whose predominant element is feeling, to the masculine poetry, whose predominant element is thought, is precisely what gives the music power over human hearts. She stoops to conquer.

With Wagner, however, the union of the two was complete ; the twain were one. The poems of his music-dramas were written by himself, and words and melodies were born together. The words, as he wrote them, immediately clothed themselves in musical phrases which he did not forget. " It is not my way," he said, " to choose a certain subject, elaborate it into verse, and then cogitate music suitable to go with it. Such a method would indeed subject me to the disadvantage of having to be inspired twice by the same subject, which is impossible. . . . Before I begin to make a verse, or even to project a scene, I am already intoxicated by the musical fragrance of my task. I have all the tones, all the characteristic motives, in my head, so that when the verses are completed and the scenes arranged, the opera is practically finished, so far as I am concerned, and the detailed execution of the work is little more than a quiet after labor which has been preceded by the real moments of creation." [1]   Of the " Siegfried " he said : " The musical phrases fit themselves on to the verses and periods without any trouble on my part; everything grows as if wild from the ground." [2]

We have here a conception of these related arts which ought to be instructive. The greatest modern master of music did not despise

[1] Quoted in Finck's *Wagner and his Works*, ii. 24.
[2] *Ibid.* p. 26.

poetry. That he could not well afford to do, for he was no mean poet. He felt that music derived its dignity, its significance, its power of impression, very largely from the poetry with which it was united. It is a question, indeed, whether he did not undervalue absolute music ; but this must be conceded, that when poetry and music are joined together, music must not be degraded by wedding it to silly words, and poetry must not be treated with contempt in the " artistic " rendering of the music. That is a truth which fits the church quite as well as the theatre ; and it is greatly to be wished that singers of hymns and anthems, as well as singers of operatic arias, would constantly bear it in mind.

The great service of Wagner was, however, the elevation of the whole conception of the music-drama. I have quoted already what he said about this in his pamphlet published before his exile. He felt that the drama, whether accompanied by music or not, ought to be a source of refinement and moral invigoration ; that it ought to suggest great thoughts and hold up high ideals. The drama was to him the queen of the arts, because it gathered into its high service architecture,

painting, poetry, and music, presenting also
in its living pictures the beauty at which sculpture aims. It must spring from the life of the
people ; and it must reflect and criticise and
idealize the life of the people ; its function is
therefore an exalted and even a sacred one.
He thought that the whole performance
ought, for this reason, to be dignified and
serious ; that the business of the artists was
not to make a spectacle of themselves, but to
represent the drama.

Far beyond this, his dramas themselves
grapple with the great themes of the spiritual
life. Their subjects are generally legendary
or mythical, because he believed that the ideal
was the field of the music-drama, and that
personalities which were symbols, rather than
historic individuals, were most serviceable. In
all these stories, however, as he tells them,
deep ethical laws are found working themselves out ; sin and its consequences, — the
retributions of violated law, and redemption
through suffering and self-sacrifice, — these
great religious ideas are presented, over and
over, with tremendous power.

Thus in the four great dramas of the "Nibelungen Ring," the tragedy which binds all

together in sorrow and fear and impending doom is the theft of the Rhine gold. It lies there in splendor at the bottom of the river; the merry Rhine daughters guard it; it is known that the possession of it will confer magical power, but it is also known that he who obtains it must renounce love. In this happy time of innocence no one wants to part with love for the sake of getting gold. But Alberich the dwarf makes that sacrifice, and Wotan, the father of the gods, is not only unwilling that he should have the gold on account of the power it bestows, but is also eager to get it to help himself out of a bad bargain with the giants, and therefore employs craft and violence to get it away from the dwarf. Thus into this primeval world come covetousness and deceit and murder and all the woes that follow in their train. The accursed thirst for gold brings curse and ruin after it. The father of the gods himself is doomed by the greed which has instigated him to gain possession of it; he is compelled by the fatal complications in which he has become involved to surrender it to the giants and they are destroyed by it. " Wotan himself," if I may adopt Hueffer's short summary, "is debarred by his promise from wrenching it from the enemy's grasp. This can only be done by the god-inspired action of a hero, who, by his own free impulse, and regardless of law, human or divine, shall restore the treasure to the depth of the Rhine. This idea of the world-redeeming power of free impulse, one might almost say of heroism, in Carlyle's sense, is the grand background on which the human events of this trilogy are inflicted; it is a tragic idea because the individual in this ideal strife must perish. In this sense Siegmund and Sieglinde, Siegfried and Brünhilde, become representatives of that pure fire of human aspiration which cannot be quenched by misfortune. They are crushed by a blind fate, but the essence of their being remains untouched by its strokes; they die, but they conquer."

There is much dispute about the meaning of Wagner's mythological parables; the expositors are not at one over the "Nibelungen Ring" any more than over the "Apocalypse," but no one can doubt that he is seriously grappling with the great questions of life and destiny.

In several of his dramas redemption is wrought by the self-sacrificing love of woman; it is the voluntary death of Senta which releases the fated Dutchman from his doom of deathless wandering; it is the love of Elizabeth, dying with a prayer on her lips for the wayward Tannhäuser, that subdues and saves him. Thus she prays for him, when he is penitent : —

> " Oh, see him meekly bending,
> Thou God of love and grace,
> Forgive thou his offending,
> And all his guilt efface ;
> For him I bend before thee,
> My life a prayer shall be,
> Make him, oh, I implore thee,
> From sin and sorrow free.
> Oh, gladly would I render
> My life for his the price,
> For him, O Lord, I tender
> My own as sacrifice."

These were strange words to hear upon the operatic stage when they were first sung there, a little more than half a century ago, — not much like the librettos of your "Traviatas" and your "Trovatores."

Not all Wagner's music-dramas are as deeply religious as "Tannhäuser;" "Die Meistersinger" is pure comedy, and "Tristan

und Isolde " is a love tragedy ; but Krehbiel
says truly that those of his dramas which, like
the Greek tragedies, are based on legendary
or mythical tales, are largely expositions of
the idea which lies at the bottom of the great
poems and dramas of Germany — " the idea
that salvation comes to humanity through the
self-sacrificing love of woman." In truth,
however, it is because he believes that the nature of woman, like the nature of music, finds
its glory and power in self-surrender, that his
dramas ascribe the work of redemption so
largely to woman.   It is the Christ-idea with
which his thought is saturated. If woman, in
most of his dramas, is the representative of
this idea, it is because he thinks that she
most perfectly represents it.

In the last, and in some respects the greatest, as it is far the most deeply religious of
his dramas, — " Parsifal," — the redeeming
work is wrought by a man.   In no other work
of dramatic art has there been such a serious attempt to incarnate the Christ-idea as in
" Parsifal." Far back in the Dresden days he
sketched a drama, " Jesus of Nazareth ; " it
was well that he waited until his riper years
and chose for the second character a form of

representation somewhat less bold. The motive of " Parsifal " is as religious as that of the miracle plays of the Middle Ages. It is not only a music-drama; the untranslatable name which he gave it, " Buhnenweihfestspiel," means, pretty nearly, " Sacred Festival Drama."

The whole tragedy of sin and punishment and redemption is here. Amfortas, King of the Holy Grail and custodian of the Sacred Spear, has been tempted and has fallen; the weapon which made him invincible has been turned against him, inflicting a remediless wound from which he must languish until a redeemer shall recover the spear and heal the hurt with its redeeming touch. Sorrow and desolation have fallen upon the whole realm on account of this transgression; the disobedience of one brings misery to many. In the midst of this troubled scene appears Parsifal, a pure innocent, who is profoundly stirred by the king's suffering, but departs, apparently unconscious of his mission. In the country of Klingsor's enchanted castle he wanders, and here, by the same temptress before whose wiles the king had fallen, he is subjected to a terrible temptation, which he resists and conquers. In this struggle with the evil his whole nature is aroused; by the swift intuition of sympathy he discerns the meaning of the conflict in which the king was worsted; his heart thrills with pity for him; he longs to save him. His victory over the evil, bought with so much struggle and suffering, makes him a captain of salvation. Because he himself has suffered, being tempted, he is able to succor them that are tempted. He is no longer the pure fool; he has learned in the school of temptation the deepest lore of the spirit. The temptress herself is humbled and saved by his resistance, and when the demon Klingsor flings at him the sacred spear, it hangs harmless in the air above his head and he seizes it and by it is made invincible. Returning with it to the country of the Grail, he heals the king's wound by a touch and delivers the nation from all its distresses.

If you wish for Wagner's interpretation of the mystery, take it in his own words: " In Parsifal the sufferings of the redeemer himself are the saving power, and at the same time the incorporation of that Ideal which the love-curse has taken from the saintly ones of the Grail Temple. Parsifal has attained unto the recognition of the sacrificial wounds of Christ, and preserving this recognition in his love of the being of his own purity, rescues the fatal spear that pierced the Saviour's side from the power of heathendom, and in conscious, compassionate sympathy heals with it the ever-bleeding wounds caused by the love-guiltiness of the deluded Grail King."

The costume of the mediæval legend is of course preserved, and much of the symbolism presents ideas which do not represent the conceptions of modern theology; but through it all these great truths shine out so clearly that the wayfaring man, though a fool, cannot miss them : that sin brings suffering and weakness and moral helplessness upon the sinner ; that from this doom he can be rescued only by one who will suffer with him, identifying himself with the sinner, and sharing his woes. There is not a hint of legal substitution in this redemption ; the vicariousness is purely moral.

When this drama was first enacted at Bayreuth a critic said : " So deeply reverent was the spirit of all the performers that the remark was made by many that the last scene of the first act was the most impressive religious service they had ever attended." No one who has seen it at Bayreuth, where alone it is given, would hesitate to offer the same testimony. It is a reverent company that witnesses it; no applause is ever tolerated; every one feels that it would be a profanation; in silence, broken only by deep breathing, the solemn scenes of the first and last acts proceed; every heart that is capable of reverential emotion is conscious that the great motives of the drama of redemption are here visibly set forth. And any one who can pass directly, as it was once my privilege to pass, from the Grand Opera at Paris, with its troops of claqueurs, its ballet injected into the heart of Gounod's "Faust," its vocal gymnastics and its clamorous calls before the curtain at the end of the scene of those who had but lately expired in our presence, — to the quiet country hill-top of Bayreuth with its darkened room, its absence of tinsel and glare, its quietly dressed and decorous assemblies, listening in hushed attention to the solemn music of "Parsifal," — would get a vivid impression of what has been done for the musical drama by the genius of Richard Wagner.

It is not to be imagined that all Wagner's musical dramas rise to this height, but this

much must be said : first, that he and no one
else has lifted the lyric stage up to a position in which work of this kind can be presented upon it; and secondly, that his entire
production is alive with ethical and spiritual conceptions. Whatever else may be said
of Richard Wagner, he is surely a great witness to the reality of the deepest truths of
morality and religion. " It is impossible,"
says Mr. Lidgey, " to study Wagner's works
without being struck by the singularly deep
religious feeling by which they are pervaded.
The broad basis of his religion was the emancipation of the human race; this was his conception of ' the fulfillment of the pure doctrine
of Christ.' To him the doctrine that Jesus
preached was Love, and in his earnest desire
to arrive at the rock of truth in religious life
and art, we cannot wonder that he felt little
or no sympathy with those who seemed to him
to have obscured that precious truth with
clouds of arbitrary and ostentatious dogma,
designed to further the worldly interests of
priesthood." [1] If we sometimes hear him
speaking with contempt of Christianity, we
must remember that it is the formal and official

[1] *Wagner,* by C. A. Lidgey, p. 85.

and not the essential Christianity at which his diatribes are directed. Upon the vital elements of the doctrine of Christ his art laid firm hold, it clothed them with the beauty of glorious music, and it will share their immortality. It is a great fact that the music-dramas of Wagner to-day dominate the lyric stage. What a mighty impulse this one man has thus given to the elevation and purification of this branch of dramatic art! If some one would do for the spoken drama what Wagner has done for the drama that is sung, the world would have deep reasons for thanksgiving.

Richard Wagner was not a saint. His temper was stormy; of tact he was destitute; he was absorbed in his own creations, and often rather oblivious of the interests of others; respecting money matters his sentiments were chivalrous, but his habits were reckless. Upon some of the episodes of his life one does not care to dwell; only the omniscient can be judges. But over against these failings we may place first his genuine democracy. To the gondolier or the cabman he was as courteous as to the king, and his servants worshiped him. To every living creature his heart went out with compassion ; there are many stories of kindness to dumb animals; his faithful dog Russ lies buried near him at Wahnfried. To his friends he was the soul of loyalty, and there were hosts of them whose devotion to him amounted to a passion.

If any one is disposed to deny that he was the greatest musician of history, that issue may well be left to the future. His work, like that of most of the great makers, is of uneven value; but when the ages to come shall have sifted the chaff from the wheat, it may appear that the largest and the best contribution to the world's store of great music at the end of the nineteenth century was the contribution of Richard Wagner.

How precious is the gift and how permanent! Paint will fade and marble crumble, but there seems to be no reason why the creations of musical art should not be just as fresh and perfect a thousand years from to-day as they are to-day. Bach and Beethoven as composers are not wrinkled and gray-headed ; their music is as young to-day as when it was written, and the perfection of instruments and of technique enables us to re-

produce it in a form far more perfect than
ever they heard it on earth. One listens
to Paderewski or Aus der Ohe playing one
of Beethoven's sonatas, or to the orchestra
under Seidl or Gericke rendering one of his
symphonies with a great longing that the
master could come back to earth and with
ears unstopped listen to his own music as we
can hear it, — how much more magnificent
than anything that ever greeted his ears while
he was in the flesh! It is a foolish wish, no
doubt, for they are playing it better, I hope,
where he is now. And I am sure that there
can never be a heaven too bright or too
happy for the Sonata Appassionata or the
Ninth Symphony, and no choir of angels that
will not delight to sing the Pilgrims' Chorus
and the Music of the Grail.

How wonderful it seems that the hand
which now lies mouldering in the sepulchre
at Wahnfried has bestowed on us so many
and so precious gifts that we can cherish
forever; has woven out of pure thought
an imperishable fabric of sweet sound, com-
mitting it to signs that are imperishable and
memorable, — so that the mind and will of
man, taking the cue thus given, can summon

at any time from the heavenly heights the
same harmonious throng; can thrill the air
of any grove or temple with the same ravish-
ing vibrations! By how many firesides, in
how many stately halls, are the strains resounding to-night which this singer first
heard and recorded — strains of quick suggestion, of uplifting thought, of ennobling
impulse!

Thanks and praise to the master who has
bequeathed to us a treasure as enduring as
time, — yea, a treasure that shall outlast
time; that memory shall forge into a golden
chain, binding the beauty of earth to the
glory of heaven!

VI

RUSKIN, THE PREACHER

The religious tone of his art treatment in "Modern Painters," is not due to a general orthodox recognition of the divine supremacy in the order of the world, still less is it to be regarded as a literary expression of youthful piety. It is the first deliberate and philosophic statement of that doctrine of theocratic government of nature and of human life, which remained a fixed principle in all his work, and which we shall perceive as dominating his conception of a sound social order. There is, indeed, a stern enthusiasm in his early statement of this creed, which bears the marks of his Calvinist ancestry, and sometimes reminds us of that famous Scottish document, the "Shorter Catechism." "Man's use and function (and let who will not grant me this follow me no further, for this I purpose always to assume) is to be the witness of the glory of God and to advance that glory by his reasonable obedience and resultant happiness." — *John A. Hobson.*

JOHN RUSKIN

VI

RUSKIN, THE PREACHER

JOHN RUSKIN was born on the 8th of February, 1819, in the heart of London. That was a notable year. Charles Kingsley, Walt Whitman, James Russell Lowell, and Queen Victoria were among those whom it gave to the world. George III. was living yet, but not reigning, and the author of the Monroe doctrine was President of the United States.

John Ruskin's family was Scotch; his father, John James Ruskin, was born in Edinburgh, and educated after the approved classical methods in the famous old High School of that city under Dr. Adam, the most distinguished of Scottish schoolmasters. In his young manhood he went to London to seek his fortune, and by dint of clear integrity and strong business sense succeeded in winning his way to the head of an important house in the wine trade. The kind of stuff of which John James Ruskin was made is indicated by a single fact.

Just as he was setting up for himself, his father failed in business with a heavy indebtedness, but the son insisted on assuming all the obligations and devoted nine years of most strenuous labor to paying off those old scores before he ever put by a penny of his own — deferring his marriage, also, until this stain upon the honor of the family could be wholly wiped away. It was not, therefore, until he was thirty-four that he was able to claim his cousin, Margaret Cox, who had waited for him all this time and would have waited longer; he carried her away from Edinburgh to the home that he had provided for her in Brunswick Square, London, and there their only child was born. "An entirely honest merchant," is the inscription which John Ruskin caused to be cut upon his father's tombstone; and a man as entirely veracious as John Ruskin would not have put it there if it had not been true. Many of us, I dare say, are not in the habit of associating high character with the traffic in which John James Ruskin was engaged; but there is abundant evidence that this man was upright and honorable; his mind, also, was finely cultivated; he was a lover and a constant reader of good books; he

was a connoisseur in pictures and a buyer of
them, too.   In all these refined tastes his wife
was at one with him ; perhaps hers was rather
the stronger nature.   Mr. Ruskin says : " My
father had the exceedingly bad habit of yield-
ing to my mother in large things, and taking
his own way in little ones." [1]   The Spartan
regimen of the household was mainly due to
Mrs. Ruskin ; the artistic ameliorations of its
severities mainly to her husband.   After John
was four years old the family removed to
Herne Hill, in Dulwich, south of the Thames,
and the manner of their life there is well preserved for us by Mr. Ruskin in " Præterita."
The Ruskins had few associates ; zealous Low
Church people as they were, they never were
absent from church on Sunday, but that was
almost their only social contact with the world
outside their garden walls.   Evenings, after
dinner, were devoted to reading ; John was
bestowed, like one of Raphael's cherubs, upon
a seat in a little niche in the wall on one side
of the chimney, and a writing table penned
him in and held his plate and cup or the book
he might be reading ; he made no trouble and
caused no interruption to the pleasure of his

[1] *Præterita*, i. 17.

parents: quite too well trained was he for that. It was a household in which the child was not spoiled by sparing the rod. He was whipped if he cried; he was whipped for carelessness if he fell down stairs: it was heroic discipline through which the child was carried; the severity, to modern judgment, seems excessive. It is an open question, however, whether modern judgment on this matter is much more sane; whether it has not traveled quite as far in the opposite direction.

Little John Ruskin, perched in his niche, and leaning in the lamplight on his table, heard much good literature, and learned to enjoy much of what he heard. " My father," he says, " was an absolutely beautiful reader of the best poetry and prose, — of Shakespeare, Pope, Spenser, Byron and Scott, as of Goldsmith, Addison and Johnson. Lighter ballad poetry he had not lightness of ear to do justice to; his sense of the strength and wisdom of true meaning and of the force of rightly ordered syllables, made his delivery of Hamlet, Lear, Cæsar or Marmion melodiously grand and just. . . . Thus I heard all the Shakespearean comedies and historical plays again and again — all Scott and 'Don Quixote,' a favorite book of my father's and at which I could then laugh in ecstasy; now it is one of the saddest, and in some things the most offensive of books." [1]

For his own reading, in these childish days, Homer, in Pope's translation, and Walter Scott were his favorite authors; but his mother compelled him to learn long chapters of the Bible by heart and " to read it every syllable through, hard names and all, from Genesis to the Apocalypse, about once a year," to which discipline he attributes his command of the resources of the English language, and whatever of vigor and beauty his style possesses. It is somewhat puzzling, however, to find him, in his maturer years, citing the 119th Psalm as most precious to him of all the Scripture that he learned in his childhood.

Another influence that told for much in the life of this child was the summer touring, for which his father's business gave the occasion. For two months every summer, with a coach and pair, Mr. Ruskin drove through England, visiting the gentry in their homes and taking orders for the supply of their wine-cellars. On these journeys, his wife and son were

[1] *Præterita*, i. 66.

always his companions, " so that," says John Ruskin, " at a jog-trot pace, and through the panoramic opening of the four windows of a post-chaise, . . . I saw all of the high roads and most of the cross-roads of England and Wales, and a great part of Lowland Scotland. . . . To my further benefit, as I grew older, I thus saw nearly all the noblemen's houses in England, in reverent and healthy delight of uncovetous admiration, perceiving, as soon as I could perceive any political truth at all, that it was probably much better to live in a small house and have Warwick Castle to be astonished at than to live in Warwick Castle and have nothing to be astonished at; but that, at all events, it would not make Brunswick Square in the least more pleasantly habitable to pull Warwick Castle down.   And, at this day, though I have kind invitations enough to visit America, I could not, even for a couple of months, live in a country so miserable as to possess no castles." [1]

All this abundance of out-of-door life was at least preparing the soil of this fertile mind for the fruit which it was yet to bear.   Nor can we wonder that a boy as delicately or-

[1] *Præterita*, i. 5, 6.

ganized as John Ruskin was, living in such
an atmosphere of books, and feasted on the
beauty of the sweetest landscapes that the sun
ever shone on, should have begun early in
life to make verses, and to exercise his powers of expression in many ways. Before he
was taught to write, he began to copy for his
own pleasure the printed type, and the amount
of literary production, in this form, with
which he is credited in his seventh and eighth
years, is notable. He gives us in " Præterita," in facsimile, some of the pages of the
books which he was producing about that
time, — manuscript books, which he made for
himself, and neatly ruled, and in which he
recorded in prose and verse his own amazing
observations and reflections. Here, for example, is a bit of a poem of two hundred and
twenty lines, composed when he was nine: —

> " Queen of flowers, O rose,
> From whose fair-colored leaves such odor flows,
> Thou must now be before thy subjects named
> Both for thy beauty and thy sweetness famed.
> Thou art the flower of England and the flower
> Of Beauty too, — of Venus' odorous bower,
> And thou wilt often shed sweet odors round,
> And often, sleeping, hide thy head on ground.
> And then the lily, towering up so proud,
> And raising its gay head among the various crowd,

There the black spots upon a scarlet ground,
And there the taper-pointed leaves are found."

Conceive of a child of nine with all that
sense of literary form ! And imagine a boy
of the same age apostrophizing Mount Skiddaw, in words like these : —

"Skiddaw, upon thy heights the sun shines bright,
But only for a moment ; then gives place
Unto a playful cloud, which on thy brow
Sports wantonly, — then floats away in air, —
Throwing its shadow on thy towering height,
And, darkening for a moment thy green side,
But adds unto its beauty, as it makes
The sun more bright when it again appears.
Then in the morning on thy brow these clouds
Rest as upon a couch, and give vain scope
For fancy's play. And airy fortresses
And towers and battlements and all appear
Chasing the others off, and in their turn
Are chased off by the others."

Frederic Harrison is not wrong in saying
that "we might pick out of 'The Excur-
sion' many a duller passage than this ; and
it would not be easy to pick a single passage
that would show the same precise and minute
watching of the clouds on a mountain, as
with the eye of a painter — the same pictorial
distinctness." [1]

Ruskin, in "Præterita," makes a careful

[1] *John Ruskin*, p. 21.

inventory of the main blessings and the chief
misfortunes of this childhood of his, and it is
a notable exhibit. Naming the good things
first, he says : " I had been taught the perfect
meaning of peace in thought, act and word.
I had never heard my father's or mother's
voice once raised in any question with each
other ; nor seen an angry or even slightly hurt
or offended glance in the eye of either."
" Next to the priceless gift of peace I had
received the perfect understanding of the nature of obedience and faith. I obeyed word
or lifted finger of father or mother as simply
as a ship obeys her helm. . . . And my practice in faith was soon complete ; nothing was
ever promised me that was not given, nothing
ever threatened me that was not inflicted, and
nothing ever told me that was not true." To
these he adds " the habit of fixed attention
with both eyes and mind," and " an extreme
perfection in palate and all other bodily
sense " due to " the utter prohibition of cake,
wine, comfits, or, except in carefullest preparation, fruit."

Now, per contra : " First, I had nothing to
love. My parents were — in a sort — visible
powers of nature to me, no more loved than

sun or the moon; only I should have been amazed and puzzled if either of them had gone out; (how much now, when both are darkened!). Still less did I love God; not that I had any quarrel with him or fear of him; but simply found what people told me was his service, disagreeable, and what people told me was his Book, not entertaining. I had no companion to quarrel with neither; nobody to assist and nobody to thank. . . . Second, of calamities I had nothing to endure. Danger or pain of any kind I knew not; my strength was never exercised, my patience never tried and my courage never fortified. . . . Thirdly I was taught no precision nor etiquette of manners; it was enough if, in the little society that we saw, I remained unobtrusive, and replied to a question without shyness. . . . Lastly and chief of evils my judgment of right and wrong and powers of independent action were left entirely undeveloped, because the bridle and the blinkers were never taken off me." [1]

It is a painful recital; I wonder whether it is quite accurate. It was written at a time when Mr. Ruskin's mind had been greatly disturbed,

[1] *Præterita*, i. 42–46.

and when his memory might have been clouded. I cannot think that love was wholly lacking in that home. Mr. Harrison, who was a frequent visitor in it, after Ruskin had come to manhood, tells us that " the relations between John and his parents were amongst the most beautiful things that will live in (his) memory ; " and that " he invariably behaved toward them with the most affectionate deference." There could not have been such affection in the deference, if there had not been a real and a recognized affection in the authority to which the deference was yielded. The whole story shows that under their stern demeanor these parents were cherishing an absorbing devotion to their only son. Yet it is evident that the child, so utterly unlike them both, craved a kind of expression of this love which was beyond their power. For the rest, Mr. Ruskin's account of the parental discipline is undoubtedly accurate, and I have dwelt on it because it is rare that a mind so wakeful and analytical as his remembers so minutely and reports so carefully the effects of parental discipline.

Under competent tutors the lad was fitted for the university ; at the age of eighteen he became a gentleman commoner of Christ

Church, Oxford, from which, six years later, he graduated. His parents had high hopes for him. " His ideal of my future," says Mr. Ruskin of his father, " now entirely formed in conviction of my genius, was that I should enter at college into the best society, take all the prizes the first year and a double first to finish with ; marry Clara Vere de Vere; write poetry as good as Byron's, only pious ; preach sermons as good as Bossuet's, only Protestant ; be made at forty Bishop of Winchester, and at fifty Primate of England." [1]

It was not only his father's hope, it was also his mother's expectation. " She had, as she solemnly told me, devoted me to God before I was born, in imitation of Hannah. Very good women," he comments, " are remarkably apt to make away with their children prematurely after this manner." [2]   The heart of this mother was perhaps reassured when this child, in his third year, on returning from church one Sunday, climbed into a chair and opened his mouth as follows : " People, be dood ! If you are dood, Dod will love you : if you are not dood, Dod will not love you. People, be dood ! "   The first sermon was,

[1] *Præterita*, i. 239.   [2] *Ibid.* p. 15.

nevertheless, ominous. It lacks the elements of sound doctrine. It puts too much stress on "mere morality." As he grew older this note was accentuated. A preacher he was likely to be — one of the greatest preachers of his century, but it became more and more clear to his own mind that he could not be a clergyman of the Church of England. His experience and that of Carlyle are parallel in this respect, though Ruskin never passed through such a struggle as Carlyle describes in "Sartor," and never, perhaps, far departed from the central beliefs of the Christian religion. Not many years ago he wrote a series of letters on the Lord's Prayer, maintaining that the essentials of religious truth are contained in it, and urging that every minister ought to make sure that every phrase in it is rightly comprehended by his people. One who takes the Lord's Prayer for his standard of doctrine cannot be far astray from the Christian way. Mr. Ruskin's theology was not formulated; like his political philosophy it was a curious mixture of radicalism and mediævalism; but the essential Christian truths were not absent from it, and he preached them, all his life long, with mighty energy of conviction.

His university course was interrupted by
serious illness, due, it would seem, to the unhappy ending of his life's first romance. One
of his father's partners in the wine business
was a French gentleman, Mr. Peter Domecq,
whose daughter Adèle had visited at the Ruskins', and John had fallen in love with her.
The young lady in no wise reciprocated the
affection ; it amused her ; she tried to laugh
him out of it, but his ardor was fanned by her
ridicule ; and when, in his third year in the
university, he learned of the betrothal of
Adèle to a French gentleman, the disappointment crushed him. There was serious pul-
monary trouble ; for a year and a half he
was fighting for his life ; his parents devoted
their whole time to him ; he was carried to
the Riviera, and sheltered and nursed until
strength returned ; finally, in 1842, when he
was twenty-three years old, he took his final
examinations.

These years had not been unproductive.
He had been constantly writing for various
periodicals, poetry chiefly ; he had won the
Newdigate prize of the university for the
best poem, and his ambitions appeared to take
this direction ; but he was deeply interested in

architecture and in painting, and among his
contributions were appreciations and criticisms
of various works of art.   Before entering the
university he had become a great admirer of
the work of Turner, and while a student he
took up the cudgels for him in some vigorous letters, signed *Kata Phusin*, the ideas
of which were afterwards expanded into his
" Modern Painters."   Of the five volumes
bearing this title the first was finished about
the time of his graduation, in 1842, and was
published anonymously the same year, when
he was twenty-three; the last was not published until 1860.   His " Seven Lamps of
Architecture," " Stones of Venice," and other
works appeared within or after these dates,
and the eloquence and beauty of this critical
and expository writing on the great themes
of art won for him immediate and wide recognition.   The opportunity thus gained was used
faithfully for the elevation of men's ideals
and the purification of their lives.   From his
particular judgments of men and their creations many deductions must be made.   He
is sometimes rash, and sometimes prejudiced ;
his generalizations are often sweeping ; but on
the whole it was a good fight for reality, for

sincerity and for spirituality in art, and the
fruits of his victory are more precious, perhaps, than most of us in these days have
known. "The law of Truth in Art," says
Mr. Harrison, "stands beside Carlyle's protest
against 'Shams.' That a building should
look what it is, and be what it is built to
serve, no one now dares dispute. That beauty
itself comes second to truth, and must be
sought in the architecture of Nature herself ;
that the art of building reflects the life and
manners, the passions and religion of those
who build ; that in building we have to consider the hands by which it is wrought ; that
art is not an end in itself, but the instrument wherein moral, intellectual, rational and
social ideals are expressed ; — all this is now
the alphabet of sound art." [1]   It was not so,
at the middle of the last century, when John
Ruskin was writing his "Seven Lamps" and
his "Stones of Venice."

Whatsoever things are pure and lovely and
true and honorable, these he sought to lift up
into the sight and admiration of men.   Art
must express life, and the life which it expresses must be sound and true and beautiful.

[1] *John Ruskin,* p. 59.

We must know the things we are dealing
with ; we must know the earth geologically ;
we must study the clouds meteorologically ;
we must know the plants and the trees and
the birds as a naturalist knows them, and tell
the truth about them ; this is the foundation
of good art. Sometimes you will take him
for a slavish realist, so sturdily does he stand
up for truth in the representation of everything ; but if you do take him that way you
will not understand him, for soon you will
hear him saying that you must be careful
about your selection, about your emphasis,
always putting that where it belongs ; that
if you tell all the truth you must tell it in
such a way as to win the admiration of men
for that which is highest.   The great school
of art, he says, " introduces in its conception
of a subject, as much beauty as is possible
consistently with truth.   For instance, in any
subject consisting of a number of figures, it
will make as many of these figures beautiful
as the faithful representation of humanity
will admit.   It will not deny the facts of
ugliness or decrepitude, or relative inferiority
or superiority of feature as necessarily manifested in a crowd, but it will, so far as it is in

its power, seek for and dwell on the beauty that is in them, not on the ugliness." [1]

Great art, he insists, is the art which tends to greaten humanity; to enlarge and ennoble the mind of the spectator, to quicken and invigorate all that is best in our nature. " I do not say," he adds, " that the art is greatest which gives most pleasure, because perhaps there is some art whose end is to teach and not to please. I do not say that the art is greatest which teaches us most, because perhaps there is some art whose end is to please and not to teach. I do not say that the art is greatest which imitates best, because perhaps there is some art whose end is to create and not to imitate. But I say that the art is greatest which conveys to the mind of the spectator by any means whatsoever, the greatest number of the greatest ideas; and I call an idea great in proportion as it is received by a higher faculty of the mind, and more fully occupies, and in occupying exercises and exalts the faculty by which it is received." [2]

The great painter, Ruskin maintains, must

[1] *Modern Painters*, iii. Part IV. ch. iii. § 12.
[2] *Ibid.* i. Part I. Sec. I. ch. ii. § 9.

be master of himself, holding intense feeling
in perfect command. It follows that " no
vain or selfish person can possibly paint, in
the noble sense of the word. Vanity and
selfishness are troublous, eager, anxious, petu-
lant; painting can only be done in calm of
mind." Equally true is it that " no shallow
or petty person can paint. It is only perfectness of mind, unity, depth, decision, the
highest qualities, in fine, of the intellect,
which will form the imagination." And
lastly " no false person can paint. A person
false at heart may, when it suits his purposes,
seize a strong truth here or there; but the
relation of truth, its perfectness, that which
makes it wholesome truth, he can never perceive. As wholeness and wholesomeness go
together, so also sight with sincerity; it is
only the constant desire of and submission to
truth which can measure its strange angles
and mark its infinite aspects and fit them and
knit them unto the strength of sacred invention." [1]

Something of that tendency to sweeping
generalization of which I spoke here appears;
it is doubtful whether, historically, the rela-

[1] *Modern Painters,* v. Part VIII. ch. iv. § 21.

tion between sound ethics and good art has always been as close as Ruskin insists. But the demands which he makes upon the artist are lofty and urgent; our highest judgment consents that this is the kind of man he ought to be. Nothing is clearer than that Ruskin conceives of his function as not one whit less sacred than that of the prophet or the minister of God; the beauty with which he is dealing is the outshining of divinity and he is to help the revelation, to be a witness for the light. Into all this art criticism no conception lower than this ever enters; it is a trumpet call to all who devote their lives to any kind of art, summoning them to rise into newness and nobility of life, to cleanse themselves from selfishness and vanity and fit themselves to be first the beholders and then the heralds of the beauty of the Lord. The foundation of this art criticism is therefore in religion; you are brought back continually to the eternal realities which underlie all existence.

And with what beauty of form is this truth arrayed! Of all the men who have used the English language John Ruskin has given us the noblest prose. It would be rewarding, if there were time, to stop and compare him with

such masters of style as Hooker, and Swift,
and Jeremy Taylor, and Macaulay, and Thackeray, and Matthew Arnold, and Hawthorne,
and Lowell, and Stevenson, and Kipling, —
all of whom have made us their debtors for
prose that charms while it instructs ; but while
I do not withhold from any of these the tribute
of my admiration, I always come back to John
Ruskin as the writer who can say things more
pithily, more keenly, more vividly, more lumi-
nously, more beautifully, more magnificently
than any one who ever wrote the English language.   There may be those who think him
too ornate ; you might say that of a sunset or
of a New England forest in October.   I wish
I could spend the rest of this hour — perhaps
I could not spend it more profitably — in repeating to you strains of this noble eloquence,
passages that I know almost by heart, but that
I never read without quickened pulses.   Many
of them are familiar to you : those words of
his about the clouds, and his exquisite descriptions of branches and leaves, of water-forms
and snow-drifts.   Take this one bit of tribute
to the beauty of mountains : —

" Consider, first, the difference produced in
the whole tone of landscape color by the intro-

duction of purple, violet, and deep ultra-
marine blue which we owe to mountains.   In
an ordinary lowland landscape we have the
blue of the sky ; the green of grass, which I
will suppose (and this is an unnecessary con-
cession to the lowlands) entirely fresh and
bright; the green of trees ; and certain elements of purple, far more rich and beautiful
than we generally should think in their bark
and shadows . . . as well as in ploughed
fields and dark ground in general.   But among
mountains, in addition to all this, large un-
broken spaces of pure violet and purple are
introduced in these distances; and even near,
by films of clouds passing over the darkness
of ravines or forests, blues are produced of
the most subtle tenderness ; these azures and
purples passing into rose-color of otherwise
wholly unattainable delicacy among the upper
summits, the blue of the sky being at the same
time purer and deeper than in the plains.
Nay, in some sense, a person who has never
seen the rose-color of dawn crossing a blue
mountain twelve or fifteen miles away can
hardly be said to know what tenderness means
at all.   Bright tenderness he may, indeed, see
in the sky or in a flower, but this grave tender-

ness of the far-away hill-purples he cannot conceive." [1]

With what power this comes home to one who loves the mountains and who can find time and chance to watch their symphonies of color in the radiant dawn and in the evening twilight. There is another passage which I find quoted by two recent biographers, Mrs. Meynell and Mr. Harrison, as illustrating the richness and splendor of Mr. Ruskin's style. It is the closing paragraph of the chapter on Lamp of Sacrifice, in the " Seven Lamps," and, happily for our purpose, deals with ornament in structural art: —

" It is one of the affectations of architects to speak of overcharged ornament. Ornament cannot be overcharged if it is good, and it is always overcharged if it is bad. . . . It is not less the boast of some styles that they can bear ornament than of others that they can do without it; but we do not often enough reflect that those very styles of so haughty simplicity, owe part of their pleasantness to contrast and would be wearisome if universal. They are but the rests and monotones of the art; it is to its far happier, far higher exalta-

[1] *Modern Painters*, iv. Part V. ch. xx. § 4.

tions that we owe those fair fronts of varie-
gated mosaic, charged with wild fancies and
dark hosts of imagery thicker and quainter than
ever filled the depth of midsummer dream;
those vaulted gates, trellised with close leaves;
those window labyrinths of twisted tracery
and starry light; those misty masses of mul-
titudinous pinnacle and diademed tower; the
only witnesses that remain to us, perhaps, of
the faith and fear of nations. All else for
which the builders sacrificed has passed away
— all their living interests, and aims, and
achievements. We know not for what they
labored, and we see no evidence of their reward. Victory, wealth, authority, happiness
— all have departed, though bought by many
a bitter sacrifice. But of them, and their toil
upon the earth, one reward, one evidence is
left us in those gray heaps of deep-wrought
stone. They have taken with them to the
grave their powers, their honors, and their errors; but they have left us their adoration."

Mrs. Meynell well says that " this splendid
passage is itself a Gothic architecture of
style," and Mr. Harrison declares that " no
man of feeling who has in him the echoes of
this funeral sermon can stand before a great

mediæval cathedral without being conscious that it has gained for him a new meaning, a sublimer pathos." Such beauty of literary form as Ruskin cultivated is not affected nowadays; yet I cannot doubt that we shall see a reaction from the stark simplicity of machine-made English, and that the color and the music of Ruskin's prose will be more highly valued in days not distant.

It was not, however, in these studies of nature and art that John Ruskin's most eloquent work was done, but rather in the prophetic teachings of the latter half of his life. For Mr. Ruskin's life divides itself into two almost exactly equal parts. Up to his fortieth year his main interest was in art; from his fortieth to his eightieth year his chief thought was given to man in his social relations. This division is by no means exclusive, for while he was studying art his eye was always upon the people to whom that art ought to furnish an uplifting ministry; " art for art's sake " he knew nothing about; art for humanity's sake was the object of his devotion. " All art," he said, " which involves no reference to man is false or nugatory. And all art which involves misconception of

man, or base thought of him, is in that degree false and base." What brought about
the change in the prevailing strain of his intellectual effort was the slowly gathering conviction that before great art could be domes-
ticated among us, society must be regenerated;
we must have better men. In the very same
year when Wagner, for his love of art, was
becoming a revolutionary, Ruskin, under the
same impulse, was girding his loins for that effort after social amelioration to which the last
half of his life was almost exclusively given.
"With your hopes for the elevation of English
art by means of frescoes [so he wrote so far
back as 1843] I cannot sympathize. . . . It
is not the material nor the space that can give
us thoughts, passions, nor power. I see on
our academy walls nothing but what is ignoble
in small pictures and would be disgusting in
great ones. It is not the love of fresco that
we want; but it is the love of God and his
creatures; it is humility and charity and self-
denial and fasting and prayer; it is a total
change of character." "So early," says Mr.
Collingwood, "he had taken up and wrapped
around him the mantle of Cassandra." [1]

[1] *Life and Work of John Ruskin*, i. 146.

What Mr. Ruskin thought he saw in the economic movements round about him was a tendency to dehumanize men. Ten years later than the letter from which I have quoted, in "The Stones of Venice," he arraigned the modern system of industry for this tendency, in words as trenchant as any he has ever written. Indeed the germ of all his teaching as a social reformer is found in that chapter on The Nature of Gothic. Hear him : —

"We have studied and much perfected of late the great civilized invention of the division of labor, only we give it a false name. It is not, truly speaking, the labor that is divided but the man. Divided into mere segments of men ; broken into small fragments and crumbs of life ; so that all the little piece of intelligence that is left in a man is not enough to make a pin or a nail, but exhausts itself in making the point of a pin or the head of a nail. Now it is a good and desirable thing, truly, to make many pins in a day ; but if we could only see with what crystal sand their points were polished — sand of human soul, much to be magnified before it could be discerned for what it is — we should think there might be some loss in it also. And the great

cry that rises from all our manufacturing cities,
louder than their furnace blast, is all in very
deed for this, — that we manufacture everything there except men; we blanch cotton, and
strengthen steel, and refine sugar, and shape
pottery, but to brighten, to strengthen, to refine or to form a single living spirit never
enters into our estimation of advantages.
And all the evil to which that cry is urging
our myriads can be met in only one way; not
by teaching nor preaching, for to teach them
is but to show them their misery, and to
preach to them, if we do nothing more than
preach, is to mock at it.   It can be met only
by a right understanding on the part of all
classes of what kinds of labor are good for
men, raising them and making them happy;
by a determined sacrifice of such convenience
or beauty or cheapness as is to be got only
by the degradation of the workman; and by
equally determined demand for the products
and results of healthy and ennobling labor." [1]

The first volume in which Mr. Ruskin set
forth his social theories was " The Political
Economy of Art," lectures delivered in Man-
chester in 1857, full of keen analysis and

[1] *Stones of Venice*, ii. vi. § 16.

pungent eloquence; after this came "Unto this Last," begun as essays in the "Cornhill Magazine" in 1860, and published as a book two years later; "Munera Pulveris," which followed in 1863; "The Crown of Wild Olive," in 1866; "Time and Tide," in 1867; and "Fors Clavigera," which was published serially, at irregular intervals, between 1871 and 1884. The violent intolerance with which the earlier of these writings were received is now almost incredible. Thackeray was the editor of "Cornhill," and the publishers of the Magazine, alarmed at the outcry against Ruskin's essays, compelled the editor to suspend their publication after four numbers had appeared. Froude, a little later, started a new series, in "Fraser's Magazine," but he, too, was forced to shut Ruskin out after the fourth number. Bigotry is not the monopoly of the religionists. There could be no more conclusive proof that such doctrine was needed than is seen in this angry determination to suppress it. Something is rotten in any alleged science which will not tolerate the free discussion of its fundamental principles. Something was rotten in the economic science of that time, and Mr. Ruskin's probe laid it open.

Needless to say his criticism was not always unerring.   Here and there it went wildly astray.   The orthodox economists could readily make this appear, and when they had exposed some glaring error in his analysis, it was easy to apply the cowardly and contemptible maxim, *ab uno disce omnia*.   To judge an argument by its flaws is the sophist's best resource.

It would be perilous for uninstructed readers to accept Mr. Ruskin as a final authority in economic science.   Not a few have done so, to their own detriment.   His attack upon profit as essentially vicious, and upon interest as morally unjustifiable, are instances of his imperfect reasoning.   He seems to assert that there can be no mutual gain in exchange; that what one party gains the other must necessarily lose.   It is true that he admits an "advantage," but refuses to call it profit, maintaining that in the transaction "nothing is constructed or produced."   Mr. Hobson's criticism is decisive.   "The orthodox economist's first comment is that something is produced by exchange, viz., utility; for things in the possession of those who need them are more useful than in the hands of those who need them less." That the method of competitive bargaining is often employed by the strong to despoil the weak is undoubtedly true, but that it is necessarily iniquitous is not true. The same defective analysis appears in his denunciations of interest. His argument rests on the assumption that "money does not grow;" it ignores the fact that money gives command of land and of capital which are productive. The prohibitions of interest in the Bible and by the ancient church refer to a wholly different state of society and to different forms of lending than those with which we are familiar. Much may be said in support of the ethical proposition that when a poor man is obliged to borrow money from a rich man to live upon, the rich man ought not to charge him interest; that was the kind of borrowing to which the Scriptural prohibitions referred. But when the money of the poor man — in the savings bank, for example — is loaned to the rich man to do business with, to employ in productive industries, there is good reason why the borrower should pay interest to the lender.

But while these and other of Mr. Ruskin's contentions have been shown to be invalid,

his attack upon the positions which the leading economists were occupying forty years
ago has been successful to a very remarkable
extent. The justification of this statement
may be shown by asking, with Mr. Hobson,
" what has now become of the maxims, ' Industry is limited by capital,' ' Labor receives
advances from a wage-fund,' ' A demand for
commodities is not a demand for labor,' ' Value
depends on cost of production,' ' Rent of land
stands by itself as a surplus, not paid out of
the product of labor, and forming no element
in price.' Is there any one of these central
dogmas of the political economy of 1860,
which commands the general allegiance of
modern teachers of commercial science? Several of them, notably the wage-fund doctrine,
and the cost theory of value, may be said to
have almost disappeared, while the others, so
far as they survive, present a strangely battered
or transformed appearance. Now, though
academic reformers of industrial science give
small attention and less credit to John Ruskin,
it is none the less true that his criticism in
' Unto this Last,' ' Munera Pulveris,' and
' Fors Clavigera ' furnishes, *in several important instances, the first clear and effective*

refutation of the mortal errors of the above-named doctrines." [1]

The central contention of Ruskin was that political economy, divorced from considerations of human welfare, is a pseudo-science; that economic questions cannot be understood apart from ethical and social questions; that the attempt to divorce them results not only in hard-hearted immorality of conduct, but in a glaringly incomplete induction of facts. The facts, he maintained, which are inexplicably involved in all production and distribution of economic goods are largely moral facts, having immediate relation to human character; to leave them out is to vitiate all your reasoning. His main thesis, perhaps, is in the words : " *There is no wealth but life,* — life, including all its powers of love, of joy, and of admiration. That country is the richest which nourishes the greatest number of noble and happy human beings. That man is the richest who, having perfected the functions of his own life to the utmost, has also the widest influence, both personal and by means of his possessions, over the lives of others. A strange political economy ; " — so

[1] *John Ruskin, Social Reformer,* p. 125.

its author himself muses— "the only one, nevertheless, that ever was or can be; all political economy founded on self-interest being but the fulfillment of that which once brought schism into the policy of angels, and ruin into the economy of heaven." [1]

This conception is steadily held and sturdily vindicated in all these books. " The real science of political economy," he urges, " is that which teaches nations to desire and labor for the things that lead to life." " Value " is that which avails for life, the life that is life indeed. Therefore the motive which the old political economy isolates and makes the centre of all its reasonings is not the central motive in any true economy. It is not the main business of any healthy human life to make money. A good soldier likes his pay, he tells the workingmen, but does not fight for money; a good clergyman does not work mainly for his fees, nor a good doctor. " And so with all other brave and highly trained men ; their work is first, their fee second — very important always, but still *second*. But in every nation, as I said, there is a vast class who are ill-educated, cowardly, and more or

---

[1] *Unto this Last*, Popular Edition, p. 126.

less stupid. And with these people, just as certainly, the fee is first and the work second, as with brave people the work is first and the fee second. And this is no small distinction. It is the whole distinction in a man ; distinction between life and death *in* him ; between heaven and hell *for* him. You cannot serve two masters. You must serve one or the other. If your work is first with you and your fee second, work is your master, and the Lord of work, who is God. But if your fee is first and your work second, fee is your master, and the Lord of fee, who is the Devil, and not only the Devil, but the lowest of devils, — ' the least erected fiend that fell.' So there you have it in brief terms : Work first, you are God's servants ; fee first, you are the fiend's. And it makes a difference, now and ever, believe me, whether you serve Him who has on his vesture and thigh written ' King of Kings,' and whose service is perfect freedom ; or him on whose vesture and thigh the name is written, ' Slave of Slaves,' and whose service is perfect slavery." [1]

These words illustrate Mr. Ruskin's power of putting plain truths pungently ; and they

[1] *The Crown of Wild Olive,* Popular Edition, p. 19.

also bear witness to the fidelity with which he preached his gospel to all sorts and conditions of men. No great teacher ever indulged less in flattery; the listening audience was sure to hear many things which were more wholesome than palatable. "Fors Clavigera" is full of the most merciless rebukes of the narrowness and ignorance of the workingmen; yet theirs was the cause for which he gave life and fortune.

It would be natural to infer that a philosopher who assailed so trenchantly the old economy and who denounced so unsparingly the existing competitive system would turn out to be a Socialist. Mr. Ruskin was, indeed, a Socialist to this extent, that he demanded a greatly increased control of industry by the State, and that he maintained the right to labor and the obligation of the State to see to it that every man has the opportunity of earning his living by his labor. But his theory of society differed very widely from that of the Socialists. He insisted that every man ought to own his own house, — ought to build it for himself, indeed; and his social scheme involved the restoration of the old system of guilds, with the return of something like feudalism. Democracy he did not believe in at all; he insisted that there were essential and everlasting differences among men, and that society must be adjusted to this fact. It is doubtful whether he ever understood the essential features of democracy; and it is clear to my own mind that much of his political teaching is inconsistent with his own deepest ethical convictions. Mr. Ruskin, as I have already said, is far from being a consistent thinker; you cannot follow him blindly. He will not let you follow him in that way. He gives you constant warnings of his fallibility. But even when you are constrained to traverse his logic, he rouses and warms you; you get much more good out of his errors than out of some men's accuracies.

The most notable enterprise of his life was his organization of the St. George's Guild, which was set on foot in the early seventies. What he chiefly desired was to withdraw the people from the great industrial towns and to teach them to live a simpler and healthier life in the country. He proposed, therefore, a fund for the purchase of agricultural land which should be cultivated by manual labor, with no steam machinery and as little as possible driven by water power, — all the laborers to be paid fixed and sufficient wages, to live in cottages of their own, their children to be educated along the lines indicated by him; manual training of the most primitive sort being central in the regimen, and outdoor sport of all varieties to be encouraged. Later he provided for the addition of an artisan class, so that the colony should be, if possible, self-maintaining. Gradually the social scheme expanded in his mind until there was quite a hierarchy of masters and marshals and landlords whose rank was fixed and whose duty it was to guide and control the companies of tenants and tradesmen and laborers. " Fors Clavigera " expounds and justifies this romantic scheme, often in passages of sinewy eloquence; and to show how serious a business it was, a most solemn declaration of faith was prepared, which every companion of the Guild was required to sign. Nothing better illustrates Mr. Ruskin's social theories than this confession and covenant : —

" I trust in the living God, Father Almighty, Maker of Heaven and Earth, and of all things and creatures, visible and invisible.

" I trust in the kindness of His law and the goodness of His work.

" And I will strive to love Him and keep His law and do His work while I live.

" I trust in the nobleness of human nature, in the majesty of its faculties, the fullness of its mercy, the joy of its love.

" And I will strive to love my neighbor as myself, and even when I cannot will act as if I did.

" I will labor, with such strength and opportunity as God gives me, for my own daily bread; and all that my hands find to do I will do with all my might.

" I will not deceive nor cause to be deceived any human being for my gain or pleasure, nor hurt, or cause to be hurt any human being for my gain or pleasure, nor rob, nor cause to be robbed any human being for my gain or pleasure.

" I will not kill or hurt any living creature needlessly, nor destroy any beautiful thing; but will strive to save and comfort all gentle life and guard and perfect all natural beauty upon the earth.

" I will strive to raise my own body and soul daily into all the higher powers of duty and happiness, not in rivalry or contention with others, but for the help, delight and honor of others, and for the joy and peace of my own life." [1]

Two other articles pledge the candidate faithfully to obey the laws of his country and the laws of his Guild. Is it not a noble hymn of faith and hope and love? If society could be organized, even in installments, on such a foundation, the millennium would be in sight. But, sad to say, the blessed day refused to dawn. Mr. Ruskin was ready with his own funds to put the scheme in operation; $50,000 was offered as a beginning and he called for volunteers who would give each a tenth of his estate to furnish the necessary capital, but the responses were few and faint. After a year or two of waiting the directors named by him acquired land in two or three places, and there was much consultation at one time with a little group of communists at Sheffield, who nibbled at the bait, but refused, when the pinch came, to go upon the land; they were doing very well as wage-workers in Sheffield and did not, after all, wish to separate themselves from the industrial system on

[1] *Fors Clavigera*, Letter lviii.

which they were waging war. So far as I can learn the plan came utterly to naught. It did not even reach the experimental stage. The Guild of St. George, about which in " Fors Clavigera " so many eloquent words were written, never materialized. One reason for the failure may have been the dangerous illness of Mr. Ruskin, from brain fever, about the time that the plans of work were maturing, — an illness from which he never fully recovered. His personal care might have saved the Guild from utter collapse. Still, all that we can say of it is, that it was a costly, perhaps a somewhat quixotic, attempt to realize his social ideals — ideals which involve a reversion to social forms that can never again be permanently reëstablished on the earth.

I have but dimly sketched the life of John Ruskin; I have failed to mention many important events and interests; I have not even spoken of his work as professor of the History of Art in Oxford, into which he threw himself for many years with great enthusiasm; nor of his connection with the Workingmen's College in London, in which he did much gratuitous teaching, devoting his great talents to the task of instructing young mechanics in

the most elementary principles of art. Nor
have I alluded to his production as an artist,
which is by no means to be despised; many of
his drawings, especially those of an architectural character, are wonderfully delicate and
spirited. I have not spoken of the bitter disappointments and sorrows of his domestic life,
in all of which he bore himself as a true and
stainless gentleman.

We often say that a writer must be judged
by his works; yet this judgment would probably be unfair to John Ruskin. We should indeed, with no misgiving, pronounce him a pure
and chivalrous soul, a man of high courage, of
unflinching truth, of unswerving devotion to
loftiest ideals. But we should also be inclined
to describe him as passionate and rude and
brusque, — a man of unamiable and turbulent
temper. In this we should do him injustice.
Those who knew him best bear witness that
the fierceness and severity which often find
utterance in his books were absent from his
personality. Mr. Harrison, who knew him well,
says: "He was the very mirror of courtesy
with an indescribable charm of spontaneous
lovingness. . . . No boy could blurt out all
that he enjoyed and wanted with more artless

freedom; no girl could be more humble, modest and unassuming. . . . The world must judge his writings as they stand. I can only say that, in personal intercourse, I have never known him, in full health, betrayed into a harsh word or an ungracious phrase, or an unkind judgment, or a trace of egotism. . . . It remains a psychological puzzle how one who could write with passion and scorn such as Carlyle and Byron never reached, who in print was so often *Athanasius contra mundum*, was in private life one of the gentlest, best, humblest of men." [1]

Mr. Ruskin inherited a fortune, something like a million dollars, and it was all expended, mainly in efforts to benefit his fellowmen. He endowed various professorships of art; he built for the common people in Sheffield, a museum which bears his name. Besides the large sums which were devoted to the Guild of St. George he did much to revive such small industries as hand weaving, wood carving, and various handicrafts. As the world measures success, he was not a successful man. And there have been many, in recent years, by whom his contribution to social

---

[1] *John Ruskin,* pp. 93-95.

science has been greatly disparaged. It needs sifting, as we have seen; but there is precious grain after the sifting, of which there shall be, in the generations following, bread of life for the nations. Mr. Harrison's inventory of what abides in Ruskin's social teaching is a legacy which most of us might be content to leave : —

"The pedantic, pseudo-scientific Plutology, or science of wealth, which he demanded, is as dead as alchemy or phlogiston. His notion that economic prosperity is subordinate to the well-being of the people is the axiom of politicians as of philosophers. His idea that the wise use of wealth, the distribution of products, the health and happiness of the producers, come before the accumulation of wealth is a commonplace, not of philanthropists but of statesmen and journalists. His appeal for organization of industry, the suppression of public nuisances and restriction of anti-social abuses, is a truism to the reformers of to-day. . . . Read all he says as to the necessity of training schools, technical schools, state supervision of practical and physical education, help to the unemployed, provision for the aged, the recovery of waste lands, the qualified ownership of the soil, . . . read all these glancings of a pure soul from heaven to earth on a multitude of things social and humane, and you will recognize how truly John Ruskin forty years ago was a pioneer of the things which to-day the best spirits of our time so earnestly yearn to see. He is forgotten now because he went forth into a sort of moral wilderness and cried, 'Repent and reform, for the kingdom of heaven is at hand.' The kingdom of heaven is not yet come on us, perhaps is yet far off; but John was the forerunner of that which will one day come to pass. He was not, as the mocking crowd said, 'a reed shaken with the wind.' "[1]

It was a long twilight, in which he rested from his labors on the shores of Coniston Water; the care of some who were dear and faithful comforted him in his declining days. For the last two years he was slowly passing under the shadow; the tablets of memory were blurred and imagination had folded her wings; the old man was an infant of days. It was mournful that one who had waited so long at the gates of the day should be left for

[1] *John Ruskin,* pp. 107, 108.

so many months in the darkness; all who loved
him gave thanks when the veil was parted
and the free spirit rose into the unfading
light. They carried his body to the grave by
the beautiful Coniston Water; hidden in
blossoms was the bier on which they bore
him; a wreath from the queen crowned the
floral offering. Men and women from all
parts of England were gathered about that
grave; if the ocean were not so wide there
would have been a far greater throng. At the
same hour, in the great Abbey at Westmin-
ster, where burial had been offered him, services were held in his memory.

Where he is we do not know; but in any
world where the glory of God is revealed
he may be confidently looked for; to discern
that glory and to open the eyes of men to
behold it has been his chief end through all
his days upon the earth. No man ever loved
the mountains better, or the evening light
upon their summits, or the clouds that kissed
and crowned them, or the forests that draped
their sides; and if, as I love to dream, the
world to which he has gone is not unlike
the world from which he has passed, then I
can almost imagine that at the advent of

one who loves them so the mountains and the hills of that country broke forth before him into singing and all the trees of the field clapped their hands.